GHOST WRITERS IN THE SKY

WHEN IT'S YOUR TIME TO COME ...

Fear not your passage
through the door, into
the glory of unobstruction,
beyond the constriction of time.
Breathe your last breath
in anticipation; for "death"
(given false connotation
of doom) is birth into life,
eternal — the natural
extension from earth to
another dimension, as
passing from room to room.

— Delma Luben

Books by Susy Smith

ADVENTURES IN THE SUPERNORMAL
THE BOOK OF JAMES
CONFESSIONS OF A PSYCHIC
THE CONVERSION OF A PSYCHIC
DO WE LIVE AFTER DEATH?
ENIGMA OF OUT-OF-BODY TRAVEL
ESP
ESP FOR THE MILLIONS
ESP & HYPNOSIS
ESP & YOU
GHOSTS AROUND THE HOUSE
GHOST WRITERS IN THE SKY
HAUNTED HOUSES FOR THE MILLIONS
HOW TO DEVELOP YOUR ESP
LIFE IS FOREVER
THE MEDIUMSHIP OF MRS. LEONARD
MORE ESP FOR THE MILLIONS
OUT-OF-BODY EXPERIENCES FOR THE MILLIONS
THE POWER OF THE MIND
PROMINENT AMERICAN GHOSTS
REINCARNATION FOR THE MILLIONS
SHE SPOKE TO THE DEAD
STRANGERS FROM SPACE
A SUPERNATURAL PRIMER FOR THE MILLIONS
SUSY SMITH'S SUPERNATURAL WORLD
TODAY'S WITCHES
VOICES OF THE DEAD?
WIDESPREAD PSYCHIC WONDERS
WORLD OF THE STRANGE

GHOST WRITERS IN THE SKY

More Communication from James

By

Susy Smith

toExcel
San Jose New York Lincoln Shanghai

Ghost Writers in the Sky

This edition published by toExcel Press,
an imprint of iUniverse.com, Inc.

For information address:
iUniverse.com, Inc.
620 North 48th Street
Suite 201
Lincoln, NE 68504-3467
www.iUniverse.com

ISBN: 1-58348-744-1

Printed in the United States of America

DEDICATED

To those who are receptive to
challenging new concepts of life
here and hereafter.

CONTENTS

CHAPTER ONE

HOW IT ALL BEGAN

To most of us life is such an ordeal that we are lucky to come out alive, but that is just what we do ... and that is the secret I wish to share. For the past thirty years I have been receiving information by what is called "automatic writing" which is a form of communication from the spirit world. My main contact is a well-known American of the last century whom I refer to as James. His name is not as important as his message; but it might nonetheless be interesting to relate here how we got together and how I eventually learned his true identity. This book then becomes a showcase for the challenging information he has given me about living here and hereafter.

On an introductory note James says: "The experience called death is not an ending but a beginning. It is an opening of doors into new and inspiring dimensions of existence. You do survive death; and, in an unbelievably exalted state, you will live forever."

Statements like this with James' many wherefores and whyfores of explanation, and his descriptions of conditions in future existence, have been the cause of my reversing completely the skeptical viewpoint with which I originally entered into my research. Hopefully they will offer glimpses of value to many of my readers.

Right now a great many people who have not previously sought answers to life's most obscure riddles are beginning to open their minds to startling new ideas. Spirit communication is a way to attain many of the explanations they seek. Undoubtedly Shirley MacLaine, with her books and television programs about her experiences with other spheres, helped start this current interest. It is evident that because she has been speaking and writing so openly, many have begun to focus their thoughts in that direction. A number of my friends and acquaintances who have never cared to read any of my other twenty-eight books about my extensive research in ESP

1

are now expressing curiosity when they learn that I am currently writing more about my psychic experiences. I've already heard a dozen times, "Be sure to let me know when the book comes out. I'm eager to read it." It is surprising and encouraging to hear this from people who used to say, "Oh, Susy, come off it. You're not really delving into all that far out stuff, are you?"

Two recent national surveys done by Rev. Andrew Greeley and his colleagues at the University of Chicago's National Opinion Research Council revealed that nearly half of American adults now believe they have been in contact with someone who has died; and two-thirds of all adults report having experienced ESP (extra-sensory perception — telepathy, clairvoyance, precognition). Fr. Greeley believes it is partly because of Shirley MacLaine and others who are now revealing an interest that millions are less afraid to face their own experiences.

So a celebrity has spoken publicly about spirit communication and aroused nationwide and perhaps worldwide interest in a subject that has existed since the beginning of time but has not been widely accepted in recent years. Discussing this current situation, James tells us: "For much too long your psychologists and behaviorists have attempted to convince you that man is a mere machine or even nothing more than a beast with a different kind of thinking apparatus. It has been forbidden by your intellectuals to discuss man as a soul or spirit living in a physical body. One has been looked on as naive if he believed in a life after death, in a soul that could continue to live forever.

"It has been evident in recent years that this idea of man as a mechanical unit has given little harmony to the world, no peace of mind, and much dissatisfaction to men, for a theory so nihilistic cannot bring happiness. Now you are beginning to realize that in order to survive as successful human beings it is necessary to have a philosophy ... to know that you are of importance in the scheme of things. There is no way you can achieve true peace of mind until you once again return to the old valid concept of man as a spirit inhabiting a body. Then you can allow yourself to conjecture about the ultimate destiny of this spirit and its reason for existing. When you finally become aware that the plan for the universe is a perfect plan and that man is a fundamental aspect of it, you will recognize your worth and that of all others."

James continued: "You survive as yourself, YOU, the person you are now; and that same individuality is always retained, even when advancing to the heights. This is because life is an unending process. The life force in everyone came from the Godhead and will always continue to exist. At your passing you leave the earth with the spiritual development already achieved to that point, not altered in any way by the transition. Nothing new has been added, and nothing has been lost except the physical body. The way your spirit grows is by your conscious effort to improve. Your goal is the highest possible spiritual advancement, which will eventually make you worthy of complete unity with God. Spiritual growth is at your own rate of speed, and all your capabilities and talents must be improved to their highest degree before you can leave the lower spheres; but eventually you will become a perfected soul living a life of eternal jubilance and service."

Learning to accept the possibility of spirit communication was a complete reversal of all my previous conditioning. As an only child born in Washington, D.C. to an Army officer and his wife, I had traveled constantly, seldom put down roots, evolved little philosophy and no religion. I was always a rationalist, never a credulous believer in anything after giving up Santa Claus and fairies and Sunday School. In college I adopted the slogan, "Always expect the worst and you won't be disappointed." I was rarely disappointed. The worst is what came to me. A brief unhappy marriage and divorce, a streptococcus blood poisoning that settled in my hip and caused me to be lame, my parents both dying and leaving me alone in the world, and much more. I've always had a naturally happy disposition so have gotten along fairly well and had many good times, but it's been in spite of what happened to me.

I majored in journalism and years later worked for a small town newspaper in Maryland, writing everything from front page articles to personals and obituaries. In 1955 I was a columnist for two newspapers in Salt Lake City, Utah. It was there that I became absorbed in survival research, and it came about because I picked up a copy of Stewart Edward White's *The Unobstructed Universe* and read his assertion that man survives death in a condition of conscious awareness and continues to live forever as himself. White also gave what appeared to be an intriguing amount of proof that he was in actual communication with his deceased wife. "Consciousness is the only reality," he said, "and consciousness is in a state of evolution." I had long favored the idea of evolution so was attracted to this thought, even though having no belief in a life after death.

Still, if there was any way that White's statements could be demonstrated scientifically, then existence would make sense to me. I had never been comfortable with descriptions of an afterlife in any of the various religions of the world, but a process of evolutionary growth after death sounded plausible. White said that our loved ones who have gone through the transition were most probably near to us and eager for us to be aware of it. The idea of communication, as he told it, would be plausible enough if there really were spirits around. If, as he insisted, our friends were still hovering about, why shouldn't they want us to know it, to relieve our grieving for them if that were the case, to assuage their own egos, for that matter, for who would want to be totally ignored all the time? Also, when they became aware of one who was in terror of the gaping void of death, wouldn't they feel an intense desire to say, "Look, it isn't like that at all. I'm still here, you'll be with me eventually, there's more to all this than meets the eye."

Just as a theory, I say, it sounded all right. But I didn't buy it. I was curious enough about it, however, that I got from the library several more of White's books on the subject and read them over a period of time. The chance that any of this might possibly be provable was enthralling to me. My daddy had been dead over twenty years. Mother only six. Was there actually a way I could try to contact them? I stopped reading and went outside to look up at Utah's beautiful Wasatch mountains for inspiration. Then I snapped a leash to the collar of my constant companion, a red miniature dachshund named Junior, and we went for a walk. And I thought many strange new thoughts, considering whether or not, in all consciousness, I ought to try to reach my parents in order to prove to myself the truth or fallacy of all this.

There, on a crisp, sunny afternoon in March, as my dog and I ambled through a large field covered with dried grasses and weeds, I was suddenly infused with a warm, loving awareness of Mother's presence. I could have reached out and hugged her — she was that close to me. She was as real and as *there* as she had been the many long ago times she'd given me my funny old teddy bear to hug and tucked me in for the night ... or the last time I tucked her in during her final illness.

This was an incredible thing to me, coming just when it did, for I'd never had such a feeling before. And life took on an immediate new dimension, which I knew it would never lose. It was a beautifully tender confirmation of the hope for survival; and no matter what happened to me in the future I would always cherish this experience and be eager if possible to recapture it.

I went back into the house with the decision to try to communicate with Mother. From then on I was a searcher, feeling myself to be on the track of something big, but unwilling for a long time to admit that there was enough evidence to convince me fully of its authenticity. So I began trying to have genuine supernormal experiences of my own in order to acquire personal conviction.

I gathered from White that the way to start this was to make efforts to communicate with spirits by using a Ouija board; and I had a friend who owned one — Veryl, a woman of absolute integrity who was just as interested as I in getting the truth. I argued with myself about whether or not to attempt it, because, remember, I didn't believe in it at all. But finally one day Veryl and I set out with Ouija for a scientific safari into the unknown. It was certainly the most unorthodox expedition in the history of research as, with board on knees and our fingers on the little heart-shaped dingus that scoots around and spells out words, Veryl and Susy moved out into uncharted territory alone and unguided.

We sat there for about ten minutes, but nothing happened except a kink in my back. So I, without the fortitude of the intrepid explorer, said, "To hell with it," and stretched out on the couch.

Veryl, remaining with the Ouija on her knees and her fingers idly resting on the pointer, suggested, "Call your mother. Maybe that will set the force in motion."

So I entreated, "Mother, if it's possible, please talk to us."

Then Veryl yelped, "Susy, come here quick!" for just as my words were spoken she had felt a sudden surge through her arm, and the pointer jumped under her hand.

5

I hurried back and sat down again and as soon as my fingers touched it, the words were spelled: "This is Mother. I ... love ... you." Then in answer to our questions, with frequent incoherencies as if Mother were having difficulty making the apparatus work for her, it told her full name, my father's name, the date of her birthday. It was interesting, but there was no way to be sure it was Mother. I could have been feeding it unconsciously. When we asked for Veryl's family, the answers were also correct; but she knew them. Although positive we weren't consciously pushing it, we were not a bit sure about anything else. Where those words were coming from was a complete enigma.

We went on for weeks trying to get evidential information from the Ouija board, but we never did. What came, though, sometimes seemed to me to be indicative of Mother's character and personality.

Once after the pointer wrote, "Betty Smith is here," I queried, "Do you know about the secret things that go on among earth people?"

The answer came, "We are so far above it that it doesn't matter."

Heaving a sigh of relief I asked Mother if she had been with me in Florida. "Yes," she answered.

Blushing a little I said, "When people do things that you used to think were naughty, do you understand why they do them?"

"Yes."

"Am I forgiven?"

"Kiss."

I took that kindly. Up until the last remark, I had been suspicious that it was my own subconscious mind doing it. But the word "Kiss" sounded just like my mother and not at all like me talking to myself.

As I said before, none of this was proof that it was Mother or that there were really spirits of the dead around to communicate, but it was a challenge to me to investigate it further, wherever the trail might lead.

I was at that time a free-lance newspaper columnist with no dependents except my little dog Junior, and I had recently inherited from a friend.enough money to support both of us for a year or two. Being able, then, to make any changes necessary in my living and working habits, I began to devote my life exclusively to seeking evidence either proving or disproving this new, enticing concept about living and dying ... and living? During the next year I traveled across the country trying to encompass everything possible about the subject, even spending most of the winter at the Parapsychology Laboratory at Duke University, learning the proper scientific approach to the psychic field. Still, wherever I was, I frequently tried to talk to Mother.

At first we continued to use the Ouija board, with only occasional success. Later I learned to do automatic writing — holding a pencil lightly to allow some invisible someone to produce messages. We wrote that way for over a year and eventually established quite a good rapport. When I asked why Daddy wasn't also there writing she told me he had already advanced to a higher plane, only visiting us occasionally.

Mother got so good at communicating that she could tell me where to find an occasional lost object and how to properly stitch a dress I was fruitlessly fashioning on the sewing machine. She even bossed me just as she used to.

Also she constantly used those old buzzwords "positive thinking" and "loving others" and insisted I reverse my cynicism and learn to apply them. I actually did begin to try.

Here is an example of the type of information which occasionally came from her. For years I had been fooling around writing my autobiography. One day I was working on a chapter about my father's adventures running away from home when he was a boy. He jumped into a boxcar, and only after the doors were closed and the train had started did he discover that there were two huge empty telephone cable spools rolling around in there. He had to jump back and forth all night to avoid being crushed by them. I wanted a word to describe his activity as some kind of lively dance and looked in *Roget's Thesaurus*, but mazurka, fandango, fling, etc. were all too commonplace. So I took pencil in hand and asked Mother for a word. She wrote "rigadoon."

I said, "Don't you mean 'brigadoon'?"

"No, rigadoon. Look it up."

The dictionary did indeed give "rigadoon, a lively dance ... it is no longer popular." It was popular with me, though, for sure. A word not even in Roget's was not likely to be in my head, so where did it come from?

Although an occasional instance of this sort continued to encourage me in my hunt for evidence, Mother and I, because she was as determined as I to get something worthwhile out of our endeavors, began a series of conversations about what it was like over there were she now lives. I had a million questions.

Then things began to get complicated, because we started to have occasional problems with unwanted spirits trying to intrude on our correspondence. I had no idea what was going on for quite a while, but eventually discovered it was those spooks who were doing silly things like making my pencil draw large circles over and over again until I was exhausted. They would write with me and claim to be Mother, or even pull my hands off the paper entirely. When they began to use vulgar language, I decided the whole thing was getting out of hand. "I've finally flipped," I wailed, and they had the nerve to agree with me.

Legitimately frightened, I gave up all efforts to write for quite a while, having realized that I was getting involved with a low type of spirit with whom I should by no means be blindly carrying on. Many who find themselves in similar situations while attempting spirit communication won't leave it alone; and dangerous things can happen to them. So the initial word everyone must always be told about any reaching out toward the unseen is DON'T unless you know exactly what you are doing. Do not follow my example and start trying to fool around with spirits without all kinds of protection and know-how. I was lucky to come out relatively sane from my innocent and unguided endeavors. Many others have not.

These kinds of entities who hang around earth and make trouble in various ways are called "earthbound", I was later to learn. They are the type who, just for devilment, interfere with someone's efforts to use Ouija boards or in other ways experiment with communication. James says of them: "An earthbound spirit is one who has led a life of no use to himself or others. He may be a crook, an unfortunate dope or alcohol addict, or even a juvenile delinquent. Or he may just be a selfish mean person who thinks he is always right. He is never anyone you would want to associate with, especially since he is invisible and able to affect you by his negative and unpleasant thoughts.

8

"For those poor individuals, existence after death is sordid and dark — nothing is beautiful to the spiritually ugly — and they may wander for centuries in a miasma of negativity. Through all this they will cling to their former customs and companions, causing untold harm to those on earth who are under their influence or whom they hated. Yes, their thoughts can be damaging, bringing all kinds of ill fortune to those who do not know they are their victims. Therefore anyone who opens himself up to their influence by making unprotected efforts at spirit communication is at risk."

I persisted, though, and until I learned to avoid them by giving up my correspondence, they gave me a taste of hell on earth. It wouldn't be nice to take the time away from James' inspirational work to talk about all my riotous experiences, but suffice it to say that for a while those mischievous entities took me on a frightening merry-go-round of mental adventures. A medium later told me, "If you were ever going to go crazy, you would already have done it because of the problems you have had in your attempts to communicate with spirits." How right she was! But somehow I toughed it out. Mother was as determined as her daughter ... stubborn dedication to a goal runs in our family. She assembled spirit helpers who tried to talk the intruders into leaving me alone, and I managed to accumulate enough good sense to listen to the wise advice of people who had been through similar situations. When I finally gave up entirely, it discouraged the bad guys, for it was no fun hanging around trying to play tricks on someone who wouldn't go frantic and scared and cuckoo. By calmly reading detective stories by the dozens to keep my mind occupied and listening to classical music and doing only routine things that were of no interest to them, I finally bored them away, I guess. Anyway, they left. But it was several months before I attempted correspondence again with mother.

I was back East then after my winter at the Parapsychology Laboratory at Duke University in North Carolina; and since it really didn't matter to me where I lived as long as mocking birds were singing in the trees there, I decided to return to Daytona Beach, Florida, where I had once spent several years and played in the surf and had a number of friends.

Impressed by the new serenity I had attained through my efforts to follow Mother's teachings, these people were eager to learn what precious substance I had mined while I'd been away so long in the West. "What happened to you?" they asked. I told them, and they really seemed interested in my experiences with the unknown. This encouraged me to resume work on the story of my life, concentrating on my efforts to communicate with spirits, and I began steadily telling it all to my typewriter.

One day it talked back.

At a loss for words as I pecked away at the erudite treatise the Preface was becoming, I slumped in my chair to relax, leaving my fingers on the keys. Then my hands began to type slowly, seemingly of their own volition. What they wrote was completely different from what I intended to say. I didn't quite like my typewriter making light of my dignified ideas this way. The book I was trying to write was supposed to have significance, yet here I was being admonished not to take myself so seriously. "Loosen up. Don't push your conclusions at your reader," my typewriter intimated. "Splash him with drops from your font of inspiration and let him brush them off or absorb them as he wishes."

After my initial surprise at being given an argument by the mechanical busybody at my fingertips, it suddenly dawned on me that Mother had found a way to talk to me again. We hadn't tried writing since I'd been scared off. Now all the intruders were gone and my receptive abilities had improved to the point that she could use the typewriter with me. After giving me information to prove that it was she, Mother indicated her interest in helping with the book in progress. We went straight to work then, and she gave out with the best data she could.

At a later date Mother turned me over to another unseen individual whom she introduced as "James Anderson." She said he knew a great deal more than she did about conditions in the world of the hereafter, having been over there much longer. She also credited him with more power to transmit his truths clearly, and she was right. When asked personal information about himself so that I could try to check whether he was a real person or some figment of my imagination, he told me a few vague facts but nothing identifiable at that time. He said he had died early in this century, that he had lived in Massachusetts, and that he'd had several children. No more exact details were given, but these turned out to be true when his real identity was revealed.

Mr. Anderson — I was quite formal with this newcomer until I got to know him — said he was interested in helping me write a book of value to those who needed to know the dangers of using Ouija boards and automatic writing without protection. Indeed, one of the reasons he wanted me as his channel was that he knew I'd personally been through such an ordeal. He said he also wanted to give the readers "this startling — to sophisticated contemporary men and women — idea that they do survive death and that therefore how they live on earth is more important than they might now realize." He added, "I will also try to show the reality of communication with those who have preceded them into the afterlife and how to use the assistance they offer. If I can get nothing more than these data into this book so that they are acceptable, I will be satisfied." Then he started addressing the reader directly, a writing technique he has continued to use frequently:

"If you have true knowledge of who you are and why you are living, you will have respect for yourself and for others, and you will be better able to adjust to the conditions of your world. When you understand that life is not just an accident, a cross one must bear for no logical reason if death brings extinction, then it will be possible to live more comfortably and think more successfully about yourself and your existence."

Mr. Anderson also wrote for my book that "Each person is an original creation. From the moment of its inception in your body, your soul (or consciousness or spirit) lives forever. Your life on earth has a purpose, a goal, a meaning — to individualize you as a person, to begin your character development, and to teach you to coexist successfully with your fellow men. Nothing occurs to anyone which cannot be a lesson, no trouble which may not produce understanding, no unhappy experience which cannot be turned into rewarding usefulness. Thus, while a pleasurable life is a gratifying goal, the acquisition of wisdom is more important. There is plenty of time later when you will be gloriously happy."

I was excited by such information as this. I felt much more power coming from Anderson, and the typewriter really smoked as he added a lot to the scanty details Mother had been able to get through to me. We worked constantly, usually far into the night, as the story about what I was learning from spirit communication took form and shape. When my invisible writing pool put their final O.K. on it as being the best we were able to accomplish at that time, I started wondering what publisher in New York to send it to. But my typewriter wrote that I would be taking it to New York myself. Mother said she knew positively that I would soon move there to live, so there was no use arguing about it.

It should be understood that I was still always fighting the premise that I was really communing with the spirits of the dead. Except for many curious incidents that seemed beyond the normal, there was never any real evidence of a scientific nature, and as a critical reporter I was determined to get facts. Yet I had already learned to listen when my typewriter talked, because conditions usually arranged themselves the way it predicted. The idea of another move had no appeal whatever. I'd always fought shy of taking on the biggest city alone, and now it seemed out of the question because there was very little money left. It was Junior who proved Mother right. He hadn't been lively for some time and I'd teased him about getting old, not suspecting that he might be ill. But suddenly his hind legs began to stiffen and he screamed with pain whenever his back was touched, so I rushed him to a vet. Shots of cortisone relieved his pain only temporarily, and the prognosis was ultimate paralysis, or else an operation which might possibly be successful.

I discovered that in Alabama, just off the road to New York, was the best veterinary college and hospital in the South, where spinal fusion operations were performed frequently on dachshunds, whose long bodies are especially prone to this disability. So I packed the car in a rush and started north well within the time prophesied. After Junior's successful laminectomy, we drove on to Virginia, where we visited friends on a rural estate for two weeks while he convalesced, and then we went on to hit the Big Apple. So within two months, there I was trying to live in New York, with no funds. I took a secretarial job in the Pathology Laboratory at Lenox Hill Hospital near the apartment I rented on East 76th Street, and wrote my priceless prose at night. Fortunately, after a few financially rough years, I began to receive grants from Eileen Garrett's Parapsychology Foundation, which subsidized my writing until I had published several books. (The manuscript I had brought with me from Daytona

Beach was finally published in 1971 under the title *Confessions of a Psychic.*)

Shortly after my arrival in New York I learned who James Anderson really was. Then I understood why he had enough wisdom and experience to be able to tell the world with conviction: "Life is by no means an accident, but a design instead; and the design is so ideal that it almost stuns you when you realize it. Prepare yourself to be stunned!"

CHAPTER TWO

THE REAL JAMES STANDS UP

It was years before I finally became convinced that I was really communicating with spirits, so at the time I first went to New York I needed all the reassurance I could get. I therefore had readings from several mediums (now frequently known as "channelers"). I never identified myself to these strangers yet was given a surprising amount of correct personal information they could not have known in a normal way. I was told among other accurate data my name and Mother's, the names of two great aunts, the fact that I was divorced, and the ever-encouraging news that I was a writer who would give the world much of inspirational value. I liked that part particularly. They frequently also mentioned the name "James" and the name "William." Finally I took an unsigned and unidentifiable page of James Anderson's script to a medium and asked him who wrote it. He put it to his forehead for inspiration and then cried, "William James! Is he your guide?"

At home after this I said to Mr. Anderson, "All right now. Out with it. Who are you really?" And he replied, "William James."

Dr. William James (1842-1910) was a prominent Harvard psychologist and philosopher for many years. His brother, the author Henry James, resided in England most of his life. William, who had a delightful sense of humor despite his serious endeavors, is especially remembered in the psychic field because he was one of the founders and the first president of the American Society for Psychical Research and also at one time president of the British Society for Psychical Research. He was an investigative thinker about the new concepts being evidenced in the study of mediumship and other phenomena.

At the time James first began to use me as a channel for his information, I would not have maintained contact with anyone who claimed to be a famous person. Mother knew this

14

because we'd already had experience with a couple of intruders giving well-known names until I called their bluff and kicked them out. I had realized even then that it is too easy for the wide-eyed to be taken in by fraudulent entities who purport to be noteworthy persons or ancient sages in order to gain an audience. So from the beginning I have been wary of famous names bandied about by spirits. That is why James decided he should come to me initially with the Anderson pseudonym.

But ever since he revealed his true identity, he has staunchly maintained that he is *the* William James and no one else. Only today as I am writing this paragraph he tells me, "I want you to insist that I am the real, the only authorized William James." The reason he is making such a point of this is because, although the first book in which I mentioned him as my communicant came out in 1967, recently other authors have published books purporting to be channeled by this same spirit. My William James denies that they are his, and they sound so different in style and content that they could hardly have come from the same source. Still, for this reason I refer to the material received from my William James primarily as "the James scripts", and I don't wave the "William" about very much. I personally now respect him highly and believe in him with all my heart, but I let his work stand on its own merit.

My friend tells me he is the head of a group of progressive schools in the world beyond the veil. Perhaps, therefore, his name has become sort of a generic term to cover almost any communicating activities of those who have been his students. Spirits who claim to be franchised, one might say, to use his name, might be the ones who communicate so widely as William James — much like the numerous Fred Astaire dancing studios in which the great Fred never tapped a toe.

Some critics have complained that none of the writings using his name sound the way the Harvard professor himself wrote when here. Why should they? In the first place, he's had innumerable new experiences. He has now progressed, he says, "as have all those who were his intellectual idols, to where they all know a great deal more than they used to when they were writing their happy little hearts out on earth."

Sometimes James gets a bit frisky and a sentence like the above comes across more like my writing style than his, but he declares they are his own words. However, a medium almost invariably unconsciously "colors" what is filtered through his mind to his voice or hands, so actually it's my fault that James' personal writing style is not evident as he runs his data by me. Those who don't know the intricacies of channeling don't understand the difficulties of getting immortal thoughts through mortal minds. A medium has to be in almost a deep trance in order for messages sent through him or her to arrive in pristine condition. And I am not even a true medium, just able to service a couple of spirits. It is as a former newspaper reporter that I've been of value to James, because he wanted to provide a clear-cut, straightforward report not prettied up with fancy prose. Very obtuse phrases don't come naturally to me; and perhaps it's just as well. Many people think if writing from alleged spirits is incomprehensible, it is particularly wise; but the language James used with me is always simple and direct, and, I'm confident, all the more profound because of it.

But why was I, Susy Smith, the one to receive this information? Mostly because I would be willing to work the long hours and years required to produce it, but also (and this is the most backhanded compliment I ever received) because, my communicant implies, I was so dumb. Actually, James says it helped that I had given up on religion and philosophy and had read almost nothing on those subjects since my college days, so my mind was like an empty sieve through which he could strain his thoughts onto the paper in front of me. I am told that one of the big problems of most spirit communication is that it has to fight the preconceived opinions of the recipient.

For years after our initial contact in Daytona Beach in the fifties, James and I wrote very little together. I was unable to take time for it, being too busy traveling around the country researching famous psychics and haunted houses and such and writing books about them.

And then came 1967 and renewed activity. In February of that year books of mine were ready to come out under the imprints of several good publishers; I was living in a small, easy-to-care-for apartment in Miami's salubrious climate, with a swimming pool outside my door for exercise and relaxation, and not unduly pressured either for time or money. I was sitting regularly once a week with a circle of friends for psychic development but was not aware if my talents had improved to any extent.

On Wednesday, February 22, I had dinner at the home of my friend Anne Fansler, and afterward we sat in meditation. Suddenly we both began to have an unusually elated feeling, as if something wonderful were about to happen. I almost burst from my skin with the joy that seized me.

Then a voice beyond my control began to speak through my lips. It didn't identify itself, but after a brief inspirational dissertation it made the statement: "You are now ready to begin receiving a book by automatic writing, and if you will be at your typewriter at nine o'clock tomorrow morning the communication will start." When my speaking apparatus was returned to me, I promised to keep the date. So, bright and early the next day I was sitting with my hands on my typewriter, expecting a rendezvous with James and not disappointed. I spent almost all of the next seven days with my fingers flying over the keys, and in that one week a first draft of the entire book was written. Witnesses were the friends who eagerly gathered each evening to hear me read the day's fresh output. Since I take a week or sometimes considerably longer to write one chapter on my own, the speed with which this came was extraordinary, to say the least.

In this book James gave a great deal more of the same type information as previously. His main premise was that because everyone survives death, how he lives on earth is the key to what his future will be like for a long, long time. So observing the proper procedures for successful spiritual growth is extremely important. The little known Natural Laws of positive thinking, loving one's fellow men, and prayer govern our lives and we should learn to use them.

James says, "Starting from life's experiences on earth and continuing in spirit planes after the transition of death, each individual is in a process of evolutionary growth, and he must eventually improve himself to the point of sublimity. The soul or consciousness of each baby born on the various inhabited planets of the universe comes from God. It enters a terrestrial body at birth to establish its identity and character, and then through eons of time in the hereafter it develops spiritually to the point that it can ultimately return in a perfected state to supplement the nucleus of Supreme Power."

A great deal was also given about conditions after death, an elaboration on the material James Anderson had given me long before. The pleasures of paradise were described as well as the wonders of the cosmos. Someone once wrote an analogy comparing the universe as seen by an enlightened spirit to a great gothic cathedral. An individual who goes into Notre Dame or Westminster Abbey at night with only a lighted match may see glimpses of the artistry around him, but he has no possible conception of the magnificence that is actually there. One who looks out onto the universe from our world is like that. In the daytime he sees a sky, sun and clouds. At night he sees a moon and twinkling stars. He does not know that in and around these tiny lights there are all kinds of beauties invisible to human eyes. James says that's the way it really is, because we can't see the wonders of other dimensions.

In order to be sure that I was receiving adequate protection from the intrusion of any negative forces, I always prayed before starting writing each day and stated firmly that nothing might approach me or in any way influence me unless it came from God in love and peace. I had also been told long before to surround myself with the White Christ Light, while picturing this powerful force encompassing me. An alternate technique James gives is, "Visualize around yourself a transparent, iridescent wall, something like a soap bubble, at arm's length from your body. Think frequently of that sheath until you succeed in feeling it around you and know that it is strong and elastic in texture. Think of it confidently as a reality, for it can become a very strong one. It is created out of actual matter, which is a substance that may be manipulated by means of thought. Although it is invisible to you, it can be seen by spirits, and no unwelcome entities can penetrate it."

After the initial reception of this text, I spent years off and on helping James edit and revise it. In and around this I wrote several books on other subjects by myself without anyone dictating to me. Finally James felt his manuscript was in good enough condition to submit to a publisher. *The Book of James* came out in hardcover (G.P. Putnam's Sons) in 1974, then in a book club edition and afterward in a Berkley paperback. Later I spent much time just answering letters, for it pulled more mail than all my other books combined. Classes were formed in Miami, Denver, Phoenix, Tucson, Los Angeles and other areas using it as a basis of teaching. Even since it went out of print I've continued to receive letters telling how helpful the James concept has been and asking how more copies can be obtained.

As an example of its value I'll tell about Kelly Niles of San Anselmo, California. Kelly is a quadriplegic — he was involved in a fist fight in a summer baseball game when he was eleven years old and has had severely restricted movement ever since. His cousin Paul is one of his helper-outers, and between them Kelly is able to laboriously type out whatever he wants to say on a small electronic communication device.

Kelly had Paul telephone and tell me that *The Book of James* had been read aloud to him a good twenty times, as it gave him hope and solace and was the best inspirational help he'd ever found. He has brought me great pleasure by phoning me at Christmas and on my birthday every year since, and sometimes in between; and it's a delight to be in touch with this remarkable young man.

After the publication of *The Book of James* there was no more contact between James and me for over five years. We probably needed a vacation from each other. Then in late February, 1979, on an impulse I sat down at my typewriter and laid my hands invitingly on the keys and guess what? James was there. We wrote together for over a period of three months, and information was received about UFOs, nuclear dangers and other topics he had not touched on previously. I'm sure my correspondent was disappointed when I terminated our writing spree in early June; but I'd had an appointment for a long time to have a total hip replacement operation, and that couldn't be ignored even for something as exciting to me as writing with James.

After this there was another long stretch — years with no writing and no contact at all between us. It seems that a rest period builds up my psychic resources, for each time I come out stronger. So I shouldn't have been surprised when I suddenly felt the urge to write this current book in the winter of 1988 to discover that James and I can now communicate without the need for the typewriter. He is able to speak through my mouth just as spirits can talk through professional mediums.

With this new capability James can now chat with me about all those statements he has made in the past; and thus he edits and modifies them by telling me to change this or that so it will be exactly as he wants it. He has also given me much new material. His main stipulation is for me to keep this book lively. He desires no dull philosophical dissertation, because, he says, this is a topic that, while profound and important, is also extremely exhilarating.

By 1978 I had retired. At least, I thought I had. And then, ten years later, when the inspiration to write *Ghost Writers in the Sky* came, suddenly I wasn't retired any more. But as I get to work again it is difficult to realize that I have been at this channeling for thirty years. It is also difficult to face the fact that in the process I have grown old.

The strange thing I've discovered is that age is very elusive. Oh, my body knows I'm older, in spades, but my mind feels just as young as ever. So here I am at seventy-eight still thinking of myself as a saucy redhead with high cheek bones and sparkly green eyes. It's a shock, I must say, to look in the mirror and see this chubby white-haired woman I hardly know.

My mother told me when she was sixty that one doesn't feel any older with the years ... that she was the same inside her mind as always. I looked at her lined face, her graying hair, her gnarled fingers and knew that behind that aging facade was the same warm, lovable wonderful woman she had always been. But a youngster? That I couldn't believe. She was right, however. Our bodies might not claim the lively persons inside, and our activities have to be limited by what we're physically able to do; but the quality of our inner lives doesn't have to change at all.

One of the handicaps of age, however, is more time off from busy, eventful living because of illness. The first week of January, 1982, I had a virus, and friends found me so sick they rushed me to Emergency, where it was revealed that my potassium was completely depleted. After a week of intravenous feeding, I left the hospital, still so weak I could hardly stand and with a terrible cough that just wouldn't quit. This lasted the entire year, during which I was in the hospital sixty-four days altogether, having IVs and antibiotics by the gallon; but nothing stopped the cough. The first of the next year a naturopathic physician put me on massive doses of vitamins and minerals that cured me within a month. But in the meantime, in July a really great incident occurred that should be related here.

When a psychic's health is poor, it is unwise to try to contact spirits, and I'd had no communication for several years. So here I was, with no word from my mother or James for a long, lonely time, coughing my lungs loose, and feeling sick and miserable. I believed my life's work was done, so why was I still hanging around on earth? I truly felt ready to give up this physical frame and get on with the next realm of existence; and to me this wasn't a negative attitude at all. On the contrary, very curious, I was eager to start my progression and see if all the things James had told me were true. I wasn't pushing it, understand, but was ready nonetheless.

One day shortly after returning from my last stay in the hospital, I was lying on the couch with the usual feeling of exhaustion, reading a gripping novel to take my mind off my discomfort. When a severe coughing attack came on, it was followed by a dark and dismal mood. There seemed no logical reason to still be hanging around here putting up with all this foolishness.

"Dear God," I started praying aloud, "please take me. Let me go over to those who love me. What good am I here? Please release me." I coughed again, a big gut-wrenching spasm. "Please, Lord, let me die," I cried out, then added quickly, "but not until I finish reading this book."

Levity was just my way of trying to show grace under pressure; but the very next mail brought me a lift that made me realize my life wasn't entirely useless as long as it was involved with James. A letter came from a stranger, Bernadine (Bernie) Krieg of Irving, Texas. She started off by saying that it had taken her a little over five and a half years to write her letter to me. She waited all that time and then by chance mailed it so I'd receive it during my only period of depression in years. Can it be merely coincidence that she finally sent it just when it was needed most?

Bernie, who was 51 in 1976 at the time of her story, told me that she and her beloved friend Bill often visited Luchea's Occult Bookstore; and one morning Bill had spent some time there roaming around among the books. Then he telephoned Bernie, suggesting she have lunch with him. She told him she'd rather just drive around with him and talk, and this turned out to be a beautiful time of verbally reaffirming their deep feelings for each other. Within an hour, at 1:40 P.M., while they were enjoying their ride together, Bill had a sudden heart attack as he drove. Bernie had the presence of mind to pull the steering wheel toward the curb and turn off the ignition. Then she called the paramedics, but Bill was dead before they reached the hospital.

This sounds like a tragic story, but it is not because of what happened next day. Bernie was drawn back to the bookstore to see if she might somehow feel closer to Bill, who had passed so quickly out of her life. She was relieved to find the place empty of customers, and, she wrote me: "I sat for a few minutes and tried to achieve a contact with him. When I felt guided, I started to slowly walk around the room. When I had almost completed the tour I heard Bill say, 'Stop!' I did, and quickly scanned the titles before me. Suddenly I found myself reaching for one — *The Book of James* by Susy Smith. The sub-title — Conversations from Beyond — seemed to be a significant message, so I turned the book over and read the information about the author on the back of the dust jacket. Above it was your picture. But, Susy, the *real* message came when I finished reading and somehow mentally received instructions to turn the book sideways."

Now who, when looking at the picture of an author and reading the blurb about her, would think to turn the book sideways, unless somehow inspired to do it? Bernie realized it was a message from her friend when she saw that the only thing to be observed when the book was turned in that fashion was the fine print along the side of my picture, crediting the photographer "Billy Mitchell, Owensboro, Kentucky." Bernie wrote of her amazement, for, "While my Love was not the man who took your picture, his name *was* Bill Mitchell, and I affectionately called him 'Billy' at times."

How could she not believe he had reached out to her to identify himself? It seems pretty likely that this man's spirit must have had a big hand in giving her the indication she needed that he still survived.

Bernie hoped I would publish this story bringing such wonderful survival evidence, and I promised to do it. Coming at the time of my deepest despondency, her letter convinced me I could continue to be of some use in the world. "I'd better hang in there after all," I thought, deciding that my time to go would have to be put on hold for a while longer.

And so now here's another book of James' philosophy, including some former material carefully edited by him and much that is new. I hope what is contained herein will stir the reader and stimulate him or her. As James says, "If we are able to impress people with the fact that they do survive death, and that they can look forward to Heaven and future lives that will be gloriously challenging and happy, then we have done the world an immense favor."

Even if you don't always agree with what James says in this book, it might not hurt to pay attention anyway, just in case.

CHAPTER THREE

GLIMPSES OF ETERNITY

I still say my prayers to "God" or "Lord" or "Dear Heavenly Father," continuing to use familiar words even though my concept of Him is greatly expanded since James widened my viewpoint by writing: "God is a Force encompassing all the highest and best in the entire universe. Every person originates from this Source, contains it within his soul, and returns to it ultimately in a sublime state. God is a Conglomerate of perfected human consciousnesses from earth and all other inhabited planets."

Hold onto your hats! There's more like this. I can only suggest that readers keep their minds open. When transcendental ideas are written by a practical, matter-of-fact individual like me, and I know they are not originating within me, it has to be faced that something supernormal is occurring. The main proof that this material is not in reality coming out of my own head is the content. How could my limited inventive abilities ever come up with an intelligent definition of God, and especially one so at variance with tradition?

As my personal contribution to this chapter, here's how I would express myself about the Deity: The only thing I know for sure about God is that He is not an ancient patriarch with a long white beard hovering in the sky to pass judgment on inhabitants of earth. And He is not a Zeus-like king with a glittering crown sitting on a throne on Mt. Olympus flinging thunderbolts at us. That is my limit. James changes these negatives into positives by stating firmly:

"When you are willing to conceive of God as a great and ever-increasing embodiment of humanity at its highest achievable state, you will understand what I am trying to say. Any definition of God that man can provide restricts Him. It may therefore be difficult for you to accept that there is an expanding God in an expanding universe, and that God expands by the addition of constantly perfected human consciousnesses. The vastness of eternity will someday be comprehensible to you, but not for a long time. Just try to accept the fact that you are part of this magnificent concept and don't worry about details that are beyond you at this point."

I was getting chills up and down my spine every time I contemplated this. James must have sensed my reaction. "Don't be appalled by your splendid journey ahead," he wrote. "Look forward to it with excitement and joy. Give God your constant love, feel your oneness with Him always, reach out to Him in prayer, but do not worry if it seems impossible to understand Him with your limited knowledge."

Now that we can talk together, I interrupted the writing with a question, because I'm as women's-lib oriented as the next modern female. "What about this 'Him' business?" I asked. "I know plenty of ladies who would like to think of God as 'Her'. I can't go writing Him/Her every time, can I? After all, the way you describe God He seems to be an amalgamation of all the hims and hers who ever lived."

"'Him' will have to do because it is the accepted way to handle such situations," James replied. "But do not get your dander up about it. I am not being chauvinistic." Then he added, "I am trying to get away from the word 'God', anyway. Because of the many incorrect anthropomorphic and mythological implications surrounding it, I am going to use it seldom from now on when I speak of the Source of All Power and Intelligence in the universe. I will instead use such terms as Ultimate Perfection, Supreme Intelligence, or Divine Consciousness."

He had used those words previously when referring to God, and I had occasionally tried since then to pray to Ultimate Perfection, Supreme Intelligence, and Divine Consciousness. It hadn't been easy. In fact, it's been almost impossible, for I am too indoctrinated in traditional praying terminology. Now, as we work on this current book I tell him this and ask him if he thinks others might not also have found those names difficult. He apparently hadn't considered that.

"Do you pray to Ultimate Perfection, Supreme Intelligence, and Divine Consciousness?" I asked him.

"Not in those words," he replied. "I know and revere Him now in those great concepts, but I still speak to Him in my prayers just as I always did all my life. I say, 'dear Lord' or 'dear God'."

"There now, see!" I crowed.

"But to refer to Him always as God all through this book is not what I want. The reader must be allowed to keep in mind the picture of God as I now know Him to be — the Great Source of All, the Ultimate Perfection!" He paused. "If you wish we will settle on that one name to use primarily in this book."

"Thanks," I said, knowing I'd have to go back through the entire manuscript and make many changes. "But just for my personal enlightenment, what do you guys on the other side call Ultimate Perfection when you refer to Him?"

"We speak of 'going to the Top' when we talk of our highest progression. It is the colloquial expression used in all of spirit land."

"I love it! But is it just flippant Americans who do this or do those of other countries also speak of going to the Top?"

"They say something like it. The Source or the Highest or the Top. Whatever it is in their languages. And we don't consider it flippant. It is merely an actuality." Then James continued writing: "No single individual on earth or progressing in spirit knows enough about Ultimate Perfection to describe Him adequately; yet there are certain attributes I may attempt to impart. He is a state, first of all, of such omnipotence, such magnificence, such magnitude, that it is impossible for us to conceive of His immensity and His greatness. Do not at any time confuse the Supreme Intelligence of the universe with man, for man is only one of His many manifestations. He is all-loving, all-powerful, all-knowing, all-seeing — all of everything. In trying for descriptive phrases that might be used, we could say that Ultimate Perfection is the State of Highest Awareness, Power Most Superlative, Illimitable Love, Infinite Consciousness. Above all He is Intelligence — inconceivable, incredible, incomprehensible intelligence. Nothing that we can in any way imagine can limit His perfection. Everything in the universe has its origin in Him and of Him. Man, himself, is an integral part of Ultimate Perfection, always has been, is now, and always will be."

James hastened to note that he is using "man" as a generic identification for both sexes, and he repeated that when he refers to God as "Him" or even Humankind as "him" it is with absolutely no sexist motives.

Emanuel Swedenborg, one of the greatest and most accomplished scientists who ever lived (he is called the most brilliant man of history) spent the last twenty-eight years of his life traveling every day to the spirit world — and no, he hadn't gone insane or become a kook. I am told that what he wrote in his many publications about his experiences was very similar to what James has given me; but I purposely have not read his works in order to protect my reception. I wouldn't want the criticism that I am crediting to James information I have acquired from other sources. So just one brief quote from him.

Swedenborg says, "Every man is an original creation." James adds to this: "Each person is a separate entity with conscious existence apart from every other, and he will always remain so." He continues that every man "will eventually progress to such heights of greatness that he achieves unity with all other men in the state of Ultimate Perfection; but this is unity in the way that members of an orchestra perform in concert or a choir sings in harmony. Souls never merge their identity into one another or into the whole. Each spirit is always an integer that knows itself to be one and individual, yet at the same time it is a functioning, self-operating, cooperating working unit in the overall Divinity.

"The pattern for man's existence, then, is this: A Soul or Conscious Awareness of Self becomes manifest at the birth of every baby born on every inhabited planet. It goes through its life cycle learning what it can from the experiences it encounters, dies to the physical body and emerges as a spirit in whatever stage of personal character development it has attained up to that time. No matter how poor a start this entity has, it will someday learn how to uplift itself and begin its joyful advancement. Eventually by its own efforts at self-improvement, and with the help of progressed spirits, it will achieve a state of wisdom and love so superlative that it enriches and increases the universe with its peace and perfection."

But what is this James keeps saying about other inhabited planets? I wanted to know and he told me.

"All the planets, stars and galaxies of the universe exist only in the cause of humanity: either for providing places of human habitation, such as earth, or as modifiers of the conditions that will make it possible for them to be habitable, such as the sun and moon. For the residents of all inhabited planets, I also use the term Man. These men may differ in their physical bodies according to situations on the planets on which they exist; but the same type consciousness that is in earth's men is in the denizens of all other worlds. Some, of course, are much more highly advanced than earthlings, mentally and spiritually, and some are less so. The physical body, no matter what form it takes, disintegrates at death and is of no more use. The consciousness of each man survives at death along with the spiritual body. Then, after the growth processes in advanced planes of existence, it attains the Heights and returns to Ultimate Perfection. The God consciousness is in each one of you no matter from which planet you come."

"If one asks James a question, one gets an answer," I said. "But sometimes it goes on and on."

He never objects to my kidding, for he knows that I revere all these wonderful insights he is revealing about God and our ultimate destinies. But our working relationship has to be on an enjoyable, friendly basis, and we often tease each other. Now he just continued writing: "It is necessary for you to comprehend the organization of the universe in order to understand anything else about it. System prevails at all times. Cause and Effect is the basic law of operation. And so if it is desired to have a new planet which will in time become inhabited, then the causes have to be set into motion to produce it. And so gases must begin to form in a certain location which will ultimately produce a sun, and then planets that will revolve around the sun are conceived and placed in their orbits. Ultimately one of these planets may produce conditions that are right for human life, and then life will be developed on it. As you suspect, this is not a hasty process. It is one that takes millions of years. But nobody is in a hurry. We are not limited by time here. Time is of your dimension, not ours."

"Time inhibits us," I said. "We live our lives by the clock."

"You will be glad to leave such obstructions as time and space," James said. "Space also is different to us than it is to you, because we move by the power of thought. Thus it is not a span of many years for us to travel from one world to another, and the farthest reaches of the universe are just a thought away. This is why it is impossible for your experts to understand the principles of space travel — because they refuse to consider the possibilities of thought power and would not know how to use it anyway.

"Inhabitants of any planet who have progressed in knowledge to the point that they understand the power of thought can use it to move about as they wish, but individuals do not attempt space travel alone. Interplanetary visitations are quite common, however, when groups use space ships, which travel vast distances quickly by using the combined thought power of all the people aboard. These machines can dematerialize to travel through space and then materialize when they reach earth, and then dematerialize again when they are ready to leave. This is why many of you have seen space ships vanish instantaneously. Also, if visitors from other worlds do not wish to land, their ship is never transformed into matter, and it may travel above you invisibly. This occurs more frequently than you know."

"Some people say," I commented, "that if extraterrestrials were real they would come down on the lawn of the White House and introduce themselves to the president. Since he's so well protected, it sounds dangerous to me; but there are those who seem to require something like this in order to believe in UFOs."

"For your sake the wise visitors from more highly advanced planets have not yet found it expedient to try to make you aware of their existence, even to bring you their advice or knowledge," was the reply. "This is because all interplanetary travelers are not benevolent. The inhabitants of some planets who are not spiritually advanced and highly civilized have nevertheless learned to use the power of thought for space travel, and they visit you on occasion, causing trouble when they appear. It is they who temporarily kidnap an occasional person or steal someone away to their home bases for experimental purposes. Be glad they are only attempting occasional night raids at present and not yet trying to land on the White House lawn or even Disneyland. It is because there is no way of your knowing the good from the bad that sagacious visitors have not yet attempted to contact your persons of importance. They think it better to keep you from getting involved with space people for a while yet."

"I don't understand why the good guys not coming would keep the bad guys away." I don't mind asking dumb questions occasionally, if it will elicit the answers needed.

"If it became the diplomatic custom to receive space people, then the rascals would be here in droves. They would be coming now if they thought you would not fight them off."

"And I suppose they'd try to take over?"

"They would at least cause unpleasant skirmishes wherever they landed."

Here James concluded the topic of unidentified flying objects; and he reverted to a recapitulation of his concept of eternity ... much more inspiring and somehow easier for me to appreciate.

"The eternal destiny for all is to exist in a state of constant blissful unity with all others in Ultimate Perfection. But it takes a long time to achieve this. You start as, one might say, a 'thought' from God, born into a physical body for the purpose of establishing your identity as one specific individual who will live forever. Whatever progress you make on earth is usually accomplished in a hit-or-miss, trial-and-error fashion because you do not realize that your object is to grow as high spiritually as possible. After the experience called death, in the next dimensions of existence, you continue your spiritual growth, but you come to know your goals and can advance by your conscious efforts at self-improvement. After many eons of time, when you are ready to attempt to reach the Heights, you are able to understand and appreciate what your place, your powers, your abilities, and your uses will be after you have perfected yourself. Then the idea of eternal life as a functioning component of Ultimate Perfection is not so appalling as it may seem to you now. It is totally inspiring and challenging ... and acceptable."

A very good friend of mine was an old gentleman named Harry Wagner who had been the founder and longtime president of the Florida Society of Psychical Research. He had a large collection of books on spiritual topics and the early psychic field, which he left to me when he died. I hadn't had time to read any of them when James and I had our three-month writing session in the spring of 1979. During this time James urged me to read this library of old books on the same general subject that he was writing with me about. "Make notes from them," he said, "and use them in the composite book we will be writing." He thought having his data backed up by other writers from long ago and far away, giving information they too had received from spirits, might help convince our readers of the truth of what he is saying.

The statements in most of these volumes I read were fairly routine, but once in a while a phrase or sentence would jump out at me that said something either identical or very similar to what James had been writing. I was quite astonished, for instance, to see in *The Aquarian Bible*: "Man is a thought of God; all thoughts of God are infinite; they are not measured up by time, for things that are concerned with time begin and end."

I had somehow presumed that Stewart Edward White had been the first to mention the idea of "evolutionary" progression after death in his 1943 book *The Unobstructed Universe* and that James had recognized the truth of it and adopted it. Yet I discovered that in 1914 W. T. Stead in *After Death* had used the term and discussed the whole concept similarly: "... death makes no break in the continuity of mental consciousness ... the principle of growth, of evolution, of endless progress towards ideal perfection, continues to be the law of life...."

Not only do many of these old-time writers agree with James, but, oddly enough, some of today's scientists are beginning to believe as well. They are fast turning into metaphysicians as they attempt to make sense of the fact that when they split the atom they discovered it to contain nothing but energy. Nonetheless it is surprising to read such a statement as the following (quoted in "Cosmic Interaction") from Dr. Evan Harris Walker, a ballistics expert and a quantum theorist, who says he sees space as inhabited by an unlimited number of interconnected conscious entities responsible for the detailed workings of the universe. "Consciousness," he says, "is everywhere."

And the eminent Cambridge biologist, Dr. Rupert Sheldrake, speaks favorably of "a creative consciousness which transcends the universe, and that is the source of its existence and of the laws that govern it."

Some astronomers today are also beginning to think of themselves as metaphysicians, as was stated on Ted Koppel's "Nightline" TV program, August 10, 1988. New telescopes have revealed that perhaps one/third of the stars in our neighborhood have planets, and, according to Professor of Earth Sciences Robert Jastrow, the conclusion would be that there is life on at least some of them. The result is that "It's an exciting time to be an astronomer."

It's also an exciting time to be writing a book that discusses many of the things people need to contemplate as they attempt truly to understand our universe.

CHAPTER FOUR

THE UNOBSTRUCTED UNIVERSE

"At death you leave your physical body behind as if you had slipped out of a coat," James tells us; "but you continue to exist in your spirit body. From your first inception, the spirit body is the pattern around which the physical body grows, so it is the real you as far as appearance and condition are concerned. It is this which survives death, accompanied by your consciousness (or soul or spirit). When you find yourself out of the physical body and in this spirit body, you may not be aware at first that any change has occurred, even though dying has caused you to move into a different dimension. You still feel the same and look the same to yourself, and you may still be at the same place you were the moment before death. You may be beside a hospital bed, at the scene of a car accident, or still lying in your own bed at home.

"I'm glad to have it confirmed that we won't suddenly find ourselves sitting on a cloud strumming a harp," I told him, speaking aloud as I usually do with James. It would be amusing for anyone to see us as we work. I frequently sit at my typewriter, often with my eyes closed even when my fingers are dancing on the keys. If I think of a question or a comment, I ask it (though not so loud the neighbors might hear and wonder). Then James answers through my mouth, so it appears that I am having a jolly good chat with myself. If the answers weren't vastly brighter than the questions, I might worry. It is reassuring that a friend who is a psychiatrist once said to me, "Whatever you are, Susy, you're not schizophrenic."

Sometimes James still types long statements. Or if I should be sitting in an easy chair reading over the scripts, I may ask a question and hear him reply, through my mouth, "Get your notebook." And then he writes with pencil. On occasions we have real conversations before he goes back to his typing or whatever. He says he likes me to interrupt from

33

time to time because it breaks his dissertations up into more palatable bits for the readers.

He answered my comment about clouds and harps by typing, "No cloud floating permitted. At first new arrivals are in the lower sphere, called the Etheric or Astral plane, which is coexistent with the earth. There is no change of place, nor change of personality immediately after death. Those of low character who have lived wickedly will find their surroundings dismal, because they are thinkers of dreary thoughts. During their earliest days in the Astral they will move around very little, always in a dark fog or gray gloom, until eventually someone in an advanced state convinces them to listen to the truth. They are told that they must change their attitude so that they can start to grow spiritually. Then eventually they will begin the progression that will take them to higher planes of existence.

"Those who were loving, kind and open-minded on earth will be in pleasant environments immediately and soon will find themselves on the upward path. There are many different spheres in the Astral, each an advancement over the others. The newcomers are told about their opportunities for growth and progress to the upper planes, and will soon be on their way to undreamed-of beauty and happiness. They learn that after they have 'graduated' from the Astral they will reach even higher dimensions of existence and that ultimately they may live anywhere in the universe they wish to be or where they find themselves useful. The culmination of such striving is reached only after a vast amount of time (in earth years, that is), but it is indeed worth the effort, because it is the state of Ultimate Perfection in which they live and work happily as units of the God Consciousness.

"All phases of spirit existence are accurately described as unobstructed' in comparison with the earth plane which is obstructed by matter," James says. "To the senses of those on earth matter is solid. To us matter is not solid. It is no obstruction to us, for we can pass right through it. Usually our biggest worry for a while after death is that you people on earth no longer see us or feel our presence. Your senses are designed for conditions in your realm, but not in ours." One of the things we are told most often, by those who have near-death experiences as well as by spirit communicants, is about the happy reunions a newcomer will have with relatives and friends who preceded him. These spirits may already have started their progression, and they tell him all the little tricks he will have to grasp in order to adjust to this strange new dimension in which he finds himself.

The first thing he has to learn is how to use his thoughts. "Until your death," James says, "it will never be possible for you to understand completely the power of thought as it is expressed in other dimensions of existence, but all activity here is by thought power. No one is able to do anything except as he conceives it mentally, because mind controls everything in the spirit world. Thought is so powerful that a reproduction of any strongly visualized object can be constructed of the degrees of energy that exist here. When we have built or originated this object with our thoughts, it actually exists and may be handled, operated, and used just as you would use a similar object that is palpable to your physical senses. We travel by thought as well. When we concentrate on any person or event on earth, we are immediately present at that locale and able to participate in what is happening, although, of course, we are invisible to mortals and they are not likely to be aware of our presence. Many of those who have begun their progression have already experienced a separation from their former world, not only mentally but spatially. This individual's progress is physical as well as mental in that distances are involved, and yet to him distance means nothing. He is as close or as far away as he thinks he is. For us the farthest reaches of the universe are but a thought away."

"Might this then explain how inhabitants of other planets travel by the speed of thought, as you said earlier?" I asked, thinking I had figured something out for once.

"No," he replied, "because they are mortal and they still have to make use of matter. They have to use the power of thought to control the physical." Because I couldn't see the difference, he added, "The matter you know on your planet is a very much slowed-down form of energy." That I could grasp, so he added, "To move their physical bodies and their space ships they handle thought power in a different manner from what we do, similar to the way you on earth have to learn to control thought power mentally."

"Okay," I said, "I'll take your word for it."

"Time is just as ephemeral here; and yet also just as real. It exists if we think of it and become involved with it; but unless we do, time does not affect us. Our sense of time is different from yours; yet you know that time also varies in your perception of it on earth."

"Do I ever," I answered him, whether I was the "you" he was talking to or not. "Time goes faster and faster for me. My birthdays get closer every year, and I don't care for that at all."

"Don't you also notice that when you are keenly interested in something time passes quickly? When you are bored it drags."

"I remember when I was little and looking forward to Christmas, December almost never passed. Yet my parents, who were busily preparing for the holidays, didn't have nearly enough time."

"Precisely," he agreed. I was sure James wanted to get on with his writing, but I had one more pertinent observation to make. "I don't know whether from your perspective you've become aware of it, but Americans today are rushing Christmas unmercifully. Advertising for it starts in October, or even before. And most of our entertaining is done before the 25th. It used to be that the week after Christmas was party week. Now almost everything is over with by Christmas night and the week afterward is used for resting, moaning over bills, and trying to pretend the whole thing never happened. I don't know why but this is a definite trend."

"It is understandable," James replied, "because advertising is the criterion for all your activities now. If you are rushed into concentrating on holiday shopping and preparations from October on, you have naturally become weary of it by the time the big day arrives and are happy to call an end to it." Then he went back to his treatise: "Time, you see, seems relative even for you. For us it is relative and no question about it. In fact, those of us who are enlightened are ordinarily unaware of the passing of time. It does not concern us because we have no need for it. The world in which we live does not depend upon the earth's revolving around the sun, or the illusion of day and night, because there is no reason for us to be so oriented. This makes it possible for us to continue to live forever without time having anything to do with it."

"It's difficult for me to think of living forever," I told him. "I envision an eternity of passing days as impossible to endure. BORING!"

"This situation does not arise with us," he replied. "We just *are*, happy and busy, and we know we will continue to be. The element of time does not enter into it."

A timeless life, James says, is much less restricting; and with no physical corporality for which to care, spirits do not have to eat or sleep and are free from the regimens and requirements of bodies that demand constant attention. "On earth there is sleeping in order to 'recharge your batteries,'" he goes on, "and dressing and undressing, cooking, sewing, cleaning or else providing the income in order to buy everything you and your family require. One of the best things that happens to us at death is this liberation from physical needs. In addition, we do not have to walk or exercise unless we want to; and it is not necessary to protect ourselves from cold or heat."

"Isn't it tiresome not to have weather?"

"We do have varying weather when we are close to earth conditions," he replied. "In higher spheres it is always moderate, sunny and delightful. If one of us decides it would be nice to enjoy a rainstorm with thunder and lightning, or a snowstorm when flakes are gently falling, we visit earth. We enjoy it, not experiencing the cold or the damp unless we wish to — which is not very likely. It is unbelievably rewarding to be free of such encumbrances of matter as getting wet, suffering from cold, or, for that matter, peeling from a sunburn.

"And yet it will be surprising to most readers, I am sure," James went on, "to learn just how many things we can do in the early stages of the Astral to make our lives similar to our previous existence. This is so that the transition between planes will be gradual enough for us to be able to accept it naturally. It must be kept in mind that you will be same person the moment after death that you were the moment before. You have the same attitudes, the same thoughts and memories, the same likes and dislikes and habits. Even if altered by illness, mental disease or senility, your personal characteristics will soon return to normal. You have now left the physical body which is no longer of use, and you will have to learn how to exist without it. In order for you not to find this overpoweringly confusing, you are permitted by the system to live in your spiritual body in similar conditions to those you previously knew, and in such close proximity to earth that you can continue to feel at home in your new environment.

"If an individual is prepared for the fact that there is no precipitate transition from living on earth to living in the next dimension and that the adaptation to the life of spirit is a gradual one, he is better able to accept it when it happens to him."

This psychiatrist friend I mentioned earlier told me that from his professional experience in counseling, he has discovered that "people need to conquer the fear of death before they are able to conquer the fear of living." It would seem to me that the easiest possible way to overcome anxiety about dying would be to know what James is telling us. Not only that we continue as ourselves after death but that the initial change from life on earth to life in spirit is not abrupt, so that we can learn to adapt as we go along. It would be awkward if at our passing we were suddenly thrust into some altogether different kind of situation to which we must adjust without knowing how to go about it.

"This transition is gradual for a very definite reason," James wrote. "Ultimate Perfection planned it that way as the most sensible and workable arrangement for man's advancement. I have originated the term 'Evolutionary Soul Progression' for this philosophy I am expounding herewith. You will find that it simplifies your concept of life if you think of it that way — as progression (or growth) of the soul of man in an evolving, step-by-step manner."

In 1955 in *You Do Take It With You* DeWitt Miller, defending the possibility of having a "second" or spiritual body, also hit on a justification for the gradual transition of which James speaks: "If we accept our survival of bodily death as proved — a conclusion which seems inescapable — then the second body is logically necessary to maintain an unbroken evolutionary chain. The very heart of evolutionary theory is the conception that progress does not take place by sudden radical changes, but rather by steady and unbroken development. That the process which developed man from amoeba and the mature individual from the infant — always by a gradual progression — should suddenly make a wild, drastic change, a change completely beyond our conception, seems highly improbable."

James went on: "God's plan for mankind often seems to you very difficult as you endure life's traumas; but the overall scheme is wise, and each step is planned so that evolutionary progression is successful. Do not fear change as it comes. Keep your hearts and your minds open and ready for exciting new adventures. I'll guarantee you will have them."

A few years back I spent the winter in Los Angeles living at the home of Barbara and Raymond Smith (no relation but good friends). In March I was scheduled to give a lecture in Las Vegas and Barb and Ray drove over with me as well as our loved mutual friend Clarissa Plantamura Mulders. Clarissa was a believer in survival of the human spirit, but she was a great seeker after *evidence* just as I had been before I succumbed to the wiles of this William James who has given me such a convincing explanation of existence without a word of legitimate proof. I spoke at the Science of Mind Church in Las Vegas; and afterward Ray, a high school teacher, said to me, "Susy, you know I don't believe in anything about spirits or a life after death. But if I did, I'd want it to be just as your James describes it."

Both Ray and Clarissa have joined the ranks on the other side since then. For some reason neither of them has ever written me to say, "Having a wonderful time. Wish you were here."

CHAPTER FIVE

THE PLEASURES OF PARADISE

Much has been written about heaven by those who have visited there like Emanuel Swedenborg or those who have had deathbed or out-of-body experiences that have offered glimpses of what life after death will be like. They make it sound beautiful, but can they give anything more than a faint impression of how magnificent it really is?

Just after a priest had given Dominic P. Sondy his last rites, at the moment doctors were hand-massaging his heart during an emergency operation for a gangrenous gall bladder, he was having the weird feeling that his eyes were leaving his head. Then they went through the ceiling and he came to a peaceful landscape of breathtaking beauty, with lovely hills, green grass and a blue cloudless sky. "All sense of time stopped," he said in *Fate* (November 1987). "The pain ceased, along with my desperate fight to stay alive. 'So this is what it's like to die,' I thought. 'Why do people fight it so much?'" A voice spoke from above his head and told him he could stay there or go back and complete his life, and since he had a wife and two children to raise he decided to return. Later his surgeon told him he had been dead for one minute.

Dr. Raymond Moody in *Life After Death* gives case histories of a similar sort. A woman he interviewed told of having died during childbirth. Immediately she saw relatives and friends she knew were already dead, and everything around her was "light and beautiful. It was a glorious moment." Sometimes people hate to leave such happiness to return to life, but fortunately she did or we would never have heard about this.

On the other hand, not everybody has such happy times. I asked James about a doctor somewhere down south who has written a book containing accounts of quite unpleasant near-death experiences. "All his patients saw was fire and brimstone," I told James. "How do you account for that."

"If those treated by this doctor thought of themselves as worthy only of hellfire after death, that is naturally what they saw," he replied. "Perhaps they were all highly religious Christian fundamentalists who believed so much in hell that they expected to reach it unless they had repented of all their sins before death."

I asked James if he minded if I used, for contrast, my favorite story which I've published several times before. He says you can't overdo something as delightful as this. Harriet M. Shelton is the pseudonym used by a dear little lady I knew in New York some years ago. She was from a wealthy family who would not have approved of a book she wrote about her psychic experiences, so used a fictitious name. She told me of several of her astral projections that I used in my book *The Enigma of Out-of-Body Travel*. They were confirmed by the Reverend Gladys Custance of Onset, Massachusetts, with whom Miss Shelton had studied clairvoyance.

On nights when Gladys and her husband, the Reverend Kenneth Custance, held meetings in Onset, Miss Shelton, who was in her New York apartment, would sometimes try to visit them by astral projection. No one at the Onset meeting knew she had any such intention the first time she attempted it on a Friday in March, 1963. But suddenly during the evening two young women cried out at the same time, "There's Miss Shelton." They actually saw her phantom. For the sake of evidence I checked with both of them and verified Miss Shelton's story. And now, with this corroborative testimony that she did have legitimate out-of-body experiences, here are her unverifiable accounts of her travels in the spirit world:

"On the planes I have visited," she told me, "the dirt roads wind along, up and down through wooded areas where the trees meet overhead. There are roadside flowers which are more vivid in color than ours, and I am told they never fade. Birds flit from tree to tree, and an occasional rabbit crosses the road ahead. Now and then a house by the roadside seems to be a replica of some much-loved home on earth. My father's Astral country place is almost an exact copy of one he had in Ridgefield." In this pleasant country Miss Shelton visited often with her parents and her deceased husband.

I asked James where these dirt roads et cetera were, and he pointed out that they could be anywhere in the universe, on earth or in space. "The whole point of it is that they are in

41

a different dimension," he said. "It is difficult for you to accept the reality of other dimensions but they definitely exist."

Among the most charming of Miss Shelton's tales are her observances of children as they enjoyed themselves running and splashing in the water, with no one fluttering about to warn them not to get hurt. The more adventurous children were diving in and out of a lake and playing under a waterfall. Then, as she stood watching them, she saw a number of youngsters running along the shore in great excitement and she realized they were having a race. "You will never believe me when I tell you," she said, "that porpoises were leaping along through the water with small boys clinging to their backs. Then, out of the woods, to my astonishment, hopped two enormous bright green frogs with boys riding them!"

"Miss Shelton had to be on Fantasy Island," I remarked to James. "Even in heaven they couldn't have pony-sized hop-toads, could they?" I'm prepared for a lot by now, but this did seem a bit far-fetched, though I found the concept delightful.

"I can tell you," he replied, "that they wouldn't grow that way naturally, but if anyone had made a special effort to devise pets or playmates that size for the children, it could be done."

The most enchanting of Miss Shelton's stories occurred when she was spending the summer in an apartment on the second floor of the Custance home in Onset. She was sitting one afternoon with Gladys when she went into trance and was taken by her spirit guide for a visit to what he called the "Animal Kingdom." There she met a handsome black-maned lion. As he walked slowly toward her, she asked her guide if it would be safe to touch him.

"Speak to him first, and see how he responds," was the answer. But this was unnecessary, for the lion came up to her and rubbed his head against her knee. Just then on the earth plane Gladys Custance's large dog Rastus burst through the door of the room in which the two ladies were sitting, and flopped down on the floor in front of his mistress' feet.

"The lion saw Rastus and walked over to him," said Miss Shelton. And Rastus saw the lion! He let out a wild yelp and tore out of the room and down the stairs like a streak. And he would never come into her apartment again.

James says, "I don't need to tell you that dogs are quite able to see animals in the spirit world if the psychic vibrations are right, and obviously they were when Miss Shelton was in a trance and a strong medium was sitting beside her."

"Whatever the conditions were, I'm all for them," I said. "Life can't help but be sweeter in a place where a lion acts just like a big old pussycat."

"It is true that beauty is in the eye of the beholder," James went on, "but when your progress begins here, your eyes are opened to all of the magical world around you. It is so overwhelming that no earthlings, not even Miss Shelton, can possibly believe what we say about the infinite variety of trees, the sparkling streams, the flowers with fragrance and color beyond all imagination. What makes it all so especially wonderful is that here happiness, peace, love, color and music are so intertwined with ravishing vistas that only blissful enjoyment is possible."

I am sure this all sounds to the reader just as beautiful and as mythical as fairyland, but James explains how all these glories occur:

"You must realize that the visions I am describing are as real and solid as anything you have on earth. They are constructed, it is true, by our thoughts, our imagings, our dreams — and those of all the millions who have passed before us — but they are material nonetheless. Although not technically exact, the best way I can explain it so you will understand is to say that they are force or energy that vibrates at much higher frequency than your mortal senses are able to apprehend. If you accept the fact that the split atom has revealed to you that all matter is energy and attempt to realize that the solid objects you see are actually composed mostly of space, why can you not envision the possibility that outer space also contains energy, and that structures similar to yours exist in a dimension you are unable to see?

"Of course, spirits are not aware of this wonderland either until they raise their thoughts to a point where it is revealed to them. None of the beauty can be perceived by those whose minds are bent only on what they already know and previously have experienced. Those earthbound souls who clutter up our space with their ignorance are only remaining close to earth because they will not lift their thoughts higher. We want them to accept what we tell them and come with us, but they

43

are stuck where they are. The time will eventually come when they will start to improve themselves, but the waste of potentially useful manpower is tremendous until then, as they remain in hellish conditions they are unable to bring themselves to leave."

"You will discuss hellfire and brimstone with me," I said, "and now you say spirits may be in hellish conditions; but you've never come right out and mentioned hell as a place. Have you anything to say about it?"

"Hell is a state of mind, not a place. Some, as you know, may experience it on earth as they continue mentally going over some terrible crimes they have committed, or sins they can't forgive. After they come here, a great many may live in hell for a long, long time, completely miserable because they are not able to raise their consciousnesses to a higher level and unwilling to attempt to undo all the harm they have done to themselves and others."

"But even they will someday progress to the heights," I stuck in, knowing for sure that he was going to say that next and wanting to show him how enlightened I had become.

James agreed, then went on with the information that the length of time it takes a spirit to advance to the heavenly state after he has once put his feet on the upward path differs with each individual. One may be so eager that he works constantly to improve himself so that he will arrive as quickly as possible to the highest areas of the Astral. "But even the happiness of heaven will not hold him for long as, ardently pursuing perfection, he leaves the Etheric and proceeds as rapidly as he can through the higher planes toward achievement of Ultimate Perfection and Eternal Bliss."

Yet we are told that even those just beginning their progression live in a beautiful world in the company of fascinating people who are doing work that is challenging and stimulating. Now James started to talk about something of which I approve heartily — good times up there. I've always said that God had to have a great sense of humor or he couldn't have devised it for us. And now we learn that heaven is indeed a happy place.

"A sense of humor is very important, and having fun is a necessary part of our development," James maintains. "We do have much gaiety, for even our work at improving ourselves is frequently arranged in the form of entertainment.

"We also have time for all the creative and constructive enterprises we were not able to work into our busy schedules on earth. Fortunately, we also have much greater clarity of mind and capacity for remembering and so our educational procedures are easier and more successful. Therefore, we can go ahead with all the academic and cultural improvements many of us always wished for but never had the time or opportunity to indulge in.

"When advancing spirits are not working helping others, being guardian angels, or in various ways trying to amount to something, they spend a good bit of their time improving their talents, and after that they may visit with friends, play games, or attend cultural affairs. Many will choose to go back to school for a time and possibly even sit at the feet of some great instructors of the past."

I said, "It would be great to sit at the feet of Plato or Abelard or any of those graybeards, but I'd be more comfortable on a bench, if you don't mind. What is best about that is the fact that after being over there a good while these teachers probably really know what they are talking about."

"Another advantage of heaven. We know whereof we speak. Much that is taught on earth, as you are aware, is conjecture. Or the limited knowledge of all those in the teaching discipline who are confident they have the answers, no matter how far from the truth they may really be.

"Over here a student may join any group he wishes. Those who are on their way upward are always welcome wherever they go. Snobbery does not exist among enlightened spirits. No one is rich while another is poor. There is no such thing as social position. All status is earned. No charge is made for anything and so each individual can afford the same as everyone else. If he does not have certain possessions, it is either because he does not want them or has not yet learned how to achieve them with his mind power."

To some new arrivals, James says, language is initially a barrier. Advanced spirits have learned to communicate entirely by telepathy, and they can talk with citizens from any country on earth or any other planets in the universe. "But when you first enter the Etheric you are untrained to use your thoughts in this manner. You are told how to employ telepathy, but it usually takes some time to assimilate this information and put it to use. So if you wish to take advantage of an interchange of ideas and information with those of other countries, you may find it expedient to spend some time studying a foreign language. You will discover real pleasure in becoming bilingual or trilingual."

We also learn that because scientific inquiry is a major concern there, some wish to attend classes or do laboratory work on any of the research projects under way — so that they can send helpful ideas to our inventors on earth.

In a book by Lillian Walbrook called *The Case of Lester Coltman* a spirit communicated the following: "My work is continued here as it began on earth, in scientific channels, and in order to pursue my studies I visit frequently a laboratory possessing extraordinarily complete facilities for carrying on of experiments. I have a home of my own, delightful in the extreme, complete with library filled with books of reference — historical, scientific, medical — and, in fact, with every type of literature. To us these books are as substantial as those used on earth are to you. I have a music room containing every mode of sound-expression. I have pictures of rare beauty and furnishings of exquisite design .... It is difficult to tell you about work in the spirit world. It is allotted to each one his portion, according to how he has progressed. If a soul has come direct from earth, or any material world, he must then be taught all he has neglected in the former existence, in order to make his character grow to perfection. As he has made those on earth suffer, so he himself suffers. If he has a great talent, that he brings to perfection here ...."

James says music is magnificent there and everyone who ever had any musical talent has discovered as he progresses that it is his obligation to himself to learn as much as he can. "It is not a matter of some kind of gatekeeper or disciplinarian standing at the entrance of the next sphere saying, 'Thou shalt not pass' until you have made the most of all your capabilities. No, it is that you, yourself, will know as you progress that you have not improved as much as possible and that there are some areas in which you have not yet achieved proper advancement. Those who have musical talents will now find the time to study, practice and participate in musical events."

This is what I'm going to do my whole first year over on the other side: "I'm gonna sing and I'm gonna dance all over God's heaven!" In fact, I'm all set for an appointment with

James to dance as much and as long as we want. It will be ballroom dancing, the fox trot, cha cha, waltz, any and all kinds of wonderful rhythmic rollicking. James says he's up to it, and I will be by the time I've gotten my old self back.

I never had much of a voice, but enough to be a second soprano in a good church choir and, quite truthfully, it was one of the most enjoyable larks of my life. So I plan to work on my voice in the next plane and get it in good shape and then join the best chorus that will have me. I'll learn to read music and then practice until invited by some really fine choir to sing Beethoven's "Ode to Joy" from his 9th Symphony and Mendelssohn's 2nd Symphony "Hymn of Praise" and even Handel's Messiah. Oh, I can hardly wait! Oh, Lordy, I hope all this James philosophy isn't just my own unconscious wishful thinking. I'm glad there's so much verification from other sources that James made me read and excerpt.

About music he was still going on: "Students are learning violin, piano, sitar, or any other instruments they choose. Advanced pupils are holding recitals. Orchestras in all stages of maturity are performing concerts. Composers who had not accomplished as much as their talents required are writing music of great beauty, and it is played by many students. You will be welcome into any recital or performance. If the program is of earth music it may be familiar to you. If it includes works by composers writing from their advanced spiritual understanding, you will enjoy music so superior to any you have ever heard before that your soul will be elevated to heights of glory as you listen.

"Another time you may visit an art exhibit where paintings and sculpture by many newcomers are being shown, along with great masterpieces by progressed spirits. I must admit that certain of your modern absurdities are not on exhibit in our heavenly planes. We have so much that is wonderful that we do not allow ourselves to be distracted by the trivial. And, it must be admitted, we do not have to think of what will sell. We have only to express the best that is within us.

"After spending a certain amount of time on your cultural improvement and development of your talents, you will perhaps then wish to play with your hobbies or games. Do you like to dance?"

I interrupted him here to cry out, "You know we love to dance! But James, this has been going on for hours! Even the spirit of Paul Bunyan would be tired after all the activities you've mapped out!"

"That is another good thing about heaven," he replied. "We never get tired here. Our stamina and interest are unlimited once we are on the upward path. You, for example, who have missed so many physical events in life because of your damaged body, will delight in endless enterprise."

Sounded good to me. But I knew nothing would ever get me to undertake the rigors of ballet dancing, and that was coming next.

"There are ballet classes for beginners as well as the more advanced, and great dancing artists are teaching those who are especially talented; but there are also many who wish to cavort just for fun without bothering to train themselves in any new routines, just continuing the steps popular in their day. Folk dancing of all countries goes on whenever groups from the same region meet. Yes, I have even seen jitterbugging here."

I am going to have to confess that I recently exposed James to dirty dancing. During a rest period after he and I had just been communicating, I turned on Oprah Winfrey's TV Show and it was featuring this newest dance craze. At my age I've outgrown sex, but I've always been quite sophisticated and little shocks me. But those kids were rubbing their bodies together in such a lascivious way that it was less like dancing than copulation. Suddenly I realized that James was there and probably still tuned in to me. "Oh, oh," I said. "Do you want me to turn this off?"

He replied, "No, I guess I ought to observe it to be aware of what's going on. You know I am attempting to remain *au courant*. It is just more evidence of the world's 'anything goes' mentality today. But it is hardly dancing. I doubt if it will play in paradise."

Yet what he was asking us to believe about pastimes in heaven could be just as horrifying to some straight-laced individuals. He has seen poker games there. With betting! But after all, the players are only wagering matchsticks or pins or money, and there is plenty more where that came from — the mind. He said they learn that outwitting their opponents at games of skill is just as exciting even without really crucial stakes. And then he admitted that bridge is also played there. "I have never heard that the problem of finding a fourth is at all prevalent here," he said. "No one, you see, has to hunt for a baby sitter, drive through traffic halfway across town, or remain at home because of illness. And no one refrains from going out for fear of being mugged.

"There are many other pleasures in spirit realms that might surprise you. I have even seen some who have come over here in recent years sitting in front of earthly television sets carefully watching your soap operas. This cannot be considered enjoyment, surely! But they do seem to relish it."

A couch potato myself, I let him ramble on anyway without interrupting. All the people who lived on earth before the advent of modern inventions will just have to get along as best they can in their heavenly haven. I may even learn to myself. Things seem to be in pretty good shape over there without videos and microwaves and computers.

James says, "Those who never missed a baseball game of their favorite teams are still attending with the human crowds at ballparks. Many spirits continue to root for their college football teams or yell and scream for their basketball [yea Arizona Wildcats!] or hockey favorites. Horse racing has its devotees also."

"I guess you know that some moralists will assume from this that you are suggesting that heaven is 'wide open,'" I admonished him.

He replied, "Instead I believe I have shown that a gradual transition from earthly pleasures to delights of a more meaningful nature is invariably successfully accomplished, and that carefree pleasure is an attribute to be encouraged. With all this, then, you will find that life is never dull after progression has begun. Advancement makes for enlightenment, and enlightenment makes for enjoyment. Every advanced spirit has a twinkling eye."

But if it will enable the reader to feel any better about it, James added, "By the time you have begun your progression, you will be spending less and less time in pursuits of an earthly nature, and those you will continue to enjoy will be even more fulfilling. Love, for instance, is not just a word to us; it is not just a feeling or an emotion. It interpenetrates us all, overwhelming us. Our attunement to it is our foremost step upward. More and more our existence is intermingled with the all-pervading love of the universe, to which human passion cannot be compared. Earthly romance or any type of affection in the Etheric plane can give us only the barest idea of the kind of overwhelming love and bliss we will experience constantly when the time comes that we finally learn to achieve our true potential, absorbing and sharing the illimitable love of Ultimate Perfection."

CHAPTER SIX

NATURAL LAWS

"The entire universe follows systems and laws," James tells us. "Nothing occurs by chance. Nothing happens by accident or in a haphazard manner, even though it may seem to. It occurs instead because of the operation of Natural Laws, which man can use even if he does not know what they are or how they operate. A good example of this is the force called electricity."

Cause and Effect is the fundamental law of the universe. And then there are the laws of Gravity, Thought Power, Love, Prayer, etc. James points out that some of these are not now accepted as natural laws; but we should not let that bother us because there is a great deal not yet known or acknowledged by science.

"These laws are always in operation and do not change," he writes. "System always prevails. Even those things that seem to be chance happenings are definitely the result of some cause, although on many occasions you are unaware of it. When you learn more about the law of cause and effect, you will understand that each event that occurs has a definite reason. Each action, a specific reaction. The great instigating power of Ultimate Perfection conceived the laws and set everything in the universe in operation in accordance with them. Order is constantly maintained. Patterns are invariably conformed to."

James concentrates on telling us about thought, love and prayer power because they are the basics, he maintains. "If you accept their reality and put them to use, very little more needs to be done to make your life successful. I know this sounds simplistic to some. There are many mystical, metaphysical and cosmic concepts that others might expect me to delve into; but let us here stay on practical paths and not go wandering into occult byways. Many aspects of existence are much too involved and complicated for us to explore in a book like this that is introductory in nature."

51

Mind is more forceful than any other power on earth, we are told. "Man can move, alter or construct objects with his thoughts when he learns to use them properly. The relationship between matter and thought is so obscure to you that it is difficult to explain how thought can affect matter, but it can be done if you will bear with me. I must first remind you that matter, while giving the illusion of solidity, is not actually solid. The nucleus of energy and the particles that move around it provide what might be called a force field of sorts, which gives the manifestation of density. But if these particles were moving at a faster rate of speed, they would not seem dense.

"As an example of what I mean: If you throw a baseball slowly, it can be seen passing through the air. If it were projected at an incredible speed, it would be invisible. Or take the blades of a fan or an airplane propeller: When moving slowly, they are visible. But when they are revved up to a high speed, you can see right through them.

"Although it is not easy for your doctors to believe this because they have found no evidence of it, the spiritual body within the physical is composed of the same force or energy as all other matter, but it is moving faster than the elements you have so far been able to identify within the atoms.

"Now thought, the strongest force in the world, is another form of energy, and it is strong enough to control the energy in matter. It can be done only by those who know how to concentrate powerfully, but it *can* be done."

I reminded James that Uri Geller, the Israeli who bends spoons, is probably the best known person doing this publicly these days; but when he performs on television, many people watching find that they too can influence objects with their minds. "As time goes on," he answered, "more and more in your sphere will probably be learning to practice mind over matter. This is an applying of one force against another, and the stronger causes the manifestation. After death use of mind power becomes more essential, but it is possible to accomplish a great deal with it on earth as well, and not just by bending or moving objects. By positive thinking every individual can change his life for the better." James gives techniques for doing this: "If you will attempt to make it a practice always and constantly to deny a negative thought the moment it appears and immediately substitute a positive one, half your battle will be won. Never for any period of time let your thoughts wander aimlessly on negative aspects of life. Alert yourself immediately to the fact that you are not only wasting time but maintaining bad conditions. Start deliberately to concentrate on something pleasant instead. Never allow yourself to dwell on a hurt or a worry. If your mind won't leave it, get very busy at any job you may have to do or go for a walk, play the piano, read a book, watch television — do anything that will take your mind off it. Nothing you do to uplift yourself makes any difference unless you think right about it. You may get up every morning and go to church, but if you sit in your pew and grieve excessively or envy someone or go over and over in your mind some insult or rebuff, you might as well have stayed at home. Mind training is not easy. But it is so well worth the trouble that it should be the first rule of operation you learn in life."

I think of James' advice so often when I catch up on the events of the day in newspapers and on television. I have learned from him never to dwell on reports about wars or terrorists or famines or other terrible things, for I tend to get upset over them. Being a news enthusiast, I continue to know what is going on, but do not let myself concentrate on the depressing information any more than I can help. Some people I know are actually miserable because the price of pork bellies has gone up, or down — whatever pork bellies do — or the political situation is not to their liking or there is more fighting in Ireland or Palestine. I used to be one of them. Now, if there is nothing I personally can do about a situation, I know it is not being callous to put it out of my mind.

It is also highly important, according to my mentor, that the power of mass opinion be recognized. Anything strongly believed by a large number of people has a definite impetus and it is necessary that its effect be understood. "Whenever one of you goes against public opinion," James says, "he is fighting an actual force as great as if he were charging into a battalion of soldiers. It is important that strongly held mass opinions that are wrong be changed, but it requires the efforts of many for long periods of time."

In *Self-Realization* magazine, summer 1973, was this little gem: "If you want to drive darkness out of a room, you don't use a fly-swatter and keep hitting at the darkness, do you?

Because even if you could do that a thousand years, you would not drive it away. The way to drive darkness out of the room is to turn on the light, or strike a match. The way to overcome your negative thinking is to apply the opposite, positive thinking."

"Yes," says James, "positive thinking may be laughed at by those who have not tried it. But the ones who practice it know that it works. They have learned from experience that it changes lives. You may live in physical discomfort and mental disharmony consistently until you learn to think constructively, then everything about your existence will alter for the better. Let no one talk you out of the necessity for positive thinking."

In line with what James is saying, I must relate a personal experience to indicate that it's better to use mind power oneself than to have it used *at* one. This happened to me once on a lecture tour when I was scheduled to speak at a club in Grosse Pointe, Michigan.

The morning of the talk there was a radio show, and the other interviewee with me was a young national official of a prominent mind-control organization. We chatted amiably before going on the air; but during the program he made the statement that he was a parapsychologist, and I impulsively and thoughtlessly challenged his use of that word. Knowing personally so many parapsychologists and having been closely involved with their work for years, I was aware that he was not one of the select clique of researchers who are very jealous of their reputation as scientific investigators of paranormal phenomena. Well, we had a bit of a set-to, and although the interview ended pleasantly enough, I had not made a friend.

That night in the large lecture hall, this man sat right straight in front of me, his eyes glinting into mine all through my talk. I was confident he was bombarding me with all the negative thoughts he knew how to use. That was the only thing I was confident of. I fumbled for words and ideas all through that grueling speech ... alone on the platform under those penetrating eyes.

James found this amusing. He always says it doesn't matter what happens to us; it's how we take it and handle it that's important.

"Did you work on trying to love that man?" he asked.

"Right while I was in the midst of lecturing? You've got to be kidding."

"That would have been a good opportunity for you to put the loving technique into practice. I am not suggesting it would have been likely for you to pause in the midst of your talk; but if you had thought of it, returning his rancorous beams with streams of pure love and benevolence would have reversed the entire situation."

"You win," I told him. "But if I ever get to the point that I can remember to do something like that, I'll believe I've reached sainthood."

"You will do that, too, someday. Love, you know, is the key to all successful spiritual growth." Then he went on with some clues for putting it into practice: "Compassion is the first step toward loving the unlovable. You can begin to feel sorry for someone you do not like or approve of, even those who do things you hate, because they do not know what a long hard road they have ahead of them spiritually. Gradually it may be possible to feel more warmly toward them and eventually to have actual love for them. Work on this, each of you men and women ... and children particularly ... for it is so important.

"Learning to love your fellow man takes consciously applied effort. Nothing in the way of spiritual growth is easy, but by concentrating on love you also learn most other quality attributes, like integrity, perseverance, honesty, etc. When you arrive over here and begin your progress toward perfection, you will have to love others all the time. It is easier if you get a head start on earth, especially when you are young; and it makes your life more successful because others will respond with love when you send it out to them. Make this a daily exercise. Whenever you discover yourself to be thinking unloving thoughts toward anyone, deny this negativity and substitute warm positive thoughts instead."

I told James, "My friend Phyllis Heald has a sign on her bathroom wall that says, 'Love your enemies. It'll drive them crazy.'"

"Don't be facetious," he replied. But I know he smiled as he went on, "Try not to judge others unkindly, and never, ever do anything deliberately to hurt anyone. All the Christian hymns, all the mantras and maxims of other religions are of no value when it is possible to allow oneself to hate or kill or maim in the name of religion, or to let others suffer poverty or hunger, or in any other way to deny them loving kindness."

A New York City acquaintance who had read some of the James scripts complained to me, "It's easy enough for disembodied spirits to talk about loving all the time, but for those of us who have to put up with the disagreeable human scum we are always rubbing elbows with, it is definitely not simple to do."

"It is no easier for us to learn to love than for you," James replied when I put her argument to him. "After all, those humans you refer to turn into spirits who are still just as disagreeable."

I stuck in, "Or as dear little Rev. Archie Matson used to say, 'If you were a weed on earth, you won't suddenly bloom into a flower in heaven.'"

"That is true. And we over here are obligated to make an effort to be kind to those weeds and try to help them and eventually learn to love them."

Would the reader believe a fellow man I once loved wrote me honest-to-goodness love letters from heaven? One day during the three-month period in the spring of 1979 while James was giving me new material, the typewriter stopped for a moment, then resumed: "Susy, this is John Metzgar. You knew I would come, didn't you?"

I had met John and dated him when I spent the fall of 1966 in Seattle, Washington, investigating a local medium. He was a hunk — nice looking, very tall and muscular, and single!

An artist who signed himself "Jonel" and painted the murals in some of Seattle's municipal buildings, John was also a non-professional hypnotist. I am somehow resistant to hypnotism (although not to hypnotists!), and that is always a challenge to those who practice this technique. John was no exception. When we first met and he was told I couldn't be hypnotized, he *knew* he was the one who could do it. And so it was arranged that he and our mutual friend Clyde Beck would visit me the next day to show me he could overcome my natural resistance to being "put to sleep" by someone else.

After they arrived I settled into a big recliner chair and John started his "You're getting sleepy...." routine. I did become completely relaxed, nestling deeper into the big chair; but John soon realized he wasn't getting anywhere with the hypnosis. I looked so cozy snuggled into the cushions, he told me later, that it seemed an invitation to him to cuddle with me. He knelt beside the chair and took me in his arms. Clyde tiptoed out of the house, John kissed me, and that was the start of something BIG. After that we had a splendid relationship, and when I left Seattle several months later we were awfully good friends.

We corresponded for a time and then, several years later, Clyde wrote me that John had been found dead on a beach in Hawaii. The authorities didn't know if it was of natural causes or a mugging. One who believes as I now do about the continuation of life in an evolutionary progression can hardly grieve when a friend dies; but there is still a real sense of loss because that eager mind, that magnificent body, that dear person has faded from view.

And now, during my first channeling period since his death, John was unexpectedly here. I was delighted, but also immediately suspicious, as I always am. I'm sorry about this, but because of my initial training in critical evaluation at the Parapsychology Laboratory, I never can help but wonder about the authenticity of my reception. As John went on to write just the things I would have wanted to hear from him, my skepticism continued; yet I was happy to think it might really be him. John wrote on three different occasions; then, shortly afterward, I terminated the entire writing session with James to have the hip operation. And that also ended my contact with my friend.

In those three letters he wrote, John gave me information I hadn't known about his death. He said: "I took a holiday to Hawaii and was alone on the beach at Hilo and went to sleep. There was nothing to it. I only hope all my friends can have such an easy time. When my mother came to greet me I was so surprised and then she finally showed me my body on the beach and people finding it and the police coming and then I realized what had happened. I am glad to be over here. I can only hope you will come soon. We'll have a good time." The writing went on to say, "I am happy to be here with you and hope to do some good writing through you. I don't know much yet, but I am certainly in good hands since I came here to you. You have many great teachers attempting to get truth through you."

About his passing, John added, "I wasn't mugged and if

they think I was they are wrong. I was there when they found my body and then I joined my mother and father and others and went away. I don't know what happened to my body after that. I wanted to start to progress right away. I have always been eager to learn, and asked my parents what I could start doing to keep me from having to come back and live another life on earth. They hadn't gone into it much, but when I decided to come and visit you I began to learn. There are many here who can teach me.

"Yes, Susy, the first thing they told me was that I will never live on earth again and that I never lived on earth before except for my one lifetime as John L. Metzgar. I gave them some argument, you can believe, but they have convinced me that I was wrong about reincarnation. I asked why so many teach it from the spirit world, and they told me that so many are teaching who don't know what they are talking about. Many spirits claim to be great master teachers whenever they find a medium or psychic who is gullible enough to believe them without question and take what they say seriously. So they say whatever they think sounds properly pompous and acceptable. They could care less if it is true."

John said something else that might be of value to readers: "Don't stop trying to get the truth to the people on earth, because it is terribly important. I wish I'd known more of the truth, but I had a good start because I was a believer. That is so important, to believe you will live after death, and then you won't be surprised at what happens to you."

John threw in a little mush here and there in his letters. I've left that out as I excerpted them here. I'm really sorry I had to stop the writing at that time, because love letters from the sky aren't easy to come by.

I am looking forward to seeing John Metzgar again when I find myself in the happy hunting ground, but not right at first. I want to have the chance to visualize myself younger and livelier again, and get my red hair back (James hasn't told me if they have beauty salons over there) before facing all my old beaux. Oh, dear, now I realize that vanity is something I'm going to have to work on.

W.T. Stead wrote in *After Death* in 1914: "Heaven is to live in the constant realization of the love of God." And James writes: "Prayer is thought power directed to the highest and best forces in the universe, your way of reaching out lovingly to Ultimate Perfection and becoming aware that He is constantly enfolding you in His loving arms.

"A prayer of mere supplication for minuscule things is not a good idea, however. It is too easy to pray for just anything you might want. But a real need should definitely be taken to the forces of good that are eager to help you. When you focus on God with calm assurance that you will be cared for, you will feel the energy and power of Ultimate Perfection flowing through you and will know that you do not stand alone. (After reading the chapter on angels and gods you will understand better the kindness and loving assistance set in operation when you pray.)"

Early in our relationship when we were in Daytona Beach, James gave me a personal pep talk: "I think you need more training in prayer. Perhaps I can give it to you. You are now aware of your contact with God, and after having been an agnostic, that is a step forward; but it would be helpful if you would spend more time in prayer. I do not mean just asking for your daily bread, but taking a moment now and then during the day to reach out to God. One never makes an effort to contact the Highest without immediately receiving love in return. If you don't feel it right at first, you will soon."

As the years went by and I transcribed James' intriguing descriptions of Ultimate Perfection, and his wise counsel about proper thinking and conduct, I began to feel more loving vibrations around me when I prayed; and eventually frequent brief prayers, particularly words of thanks, began to seem the natural thing to do. James recognized this when he spoke to me about it during the script writing in 1979: "It is good that you have learned to pray more. You have come a long way since I have known you. As time goes by I see a difference in your attitude towards others as well. You are much less critical than you used to be."

Today he tells me: "You are still not what I would call a traditional pray-er. You go at it by fits and starts in bits and pieces. And yet you have results in the joy you feel and the security you know from having placed yourself in God's hands. Each person has his own way of praying and just doing it is the most important thing. Being receptive to God's love can bring happiness in everyone's lives."

As James concludes his discussion of Natural Laws he writes: "Prayer is thought power directed to the universal Source of all power. It cannot help but be successful, for it is putting into effect the strongest of all forces and directing them toward the highest and mightiest energies of the universe. As you reveal in your lives the results of knowing the love of Ultimate Perfection, you become aware that prayer works. Love works. Thought power works."

CHAPTER SEVEN

HERE THERE BE TURTLES

Uri Geller, the Israeli sensitive widely known for using mind power to affect physical objects, has been tested many times, many places by many critical researchers.

Dr. Ted Bastin, a physics professor of Cambridge University, is quoted in *Psychic* (June, 1973) as saying: "The things I have seen him do are quite remarkable ... bending metal objects without ever actually touching them, and moving objects across rooms. This is a phenomenon we have stumbled across that might blow apart the reigning orthodox scientific views."

Astronaut-turned-parapsychologist Captain Edgar Mitchell has observed Geller frequently and he reports: "In addition to the rigidly controlled experimental work that has been done with Uri Geller ... there are many startling events that take place when he is around and in the proper state of mind. An evening with Geller is likely to produce an assortment of bent rings, bent and broken silverware, mysteriously lost articles and mysteriously found articles. For example, it is not unusual to see Uri pick up a normal spoon to stir his coffee and have the spoon come out of the coffee twisted or broken .... On one particular evening, approximately twenty such bizarre events ... took place in less than three hours, in the presence of three well-qualified observers."

Uri Geller performed in Phoenix, Arizona, a few years ago and to attend I drove up from my home in Tucson with a party of six men and women who were computer analysts at Kitt Peak Observatory. First we had dinner at a nice restaurant, and during the meal someone said, "Did you all bring teaspoons?" We'd been forewarned that during his performances Uri sometimes bent those held by members of his audience.

"I forgot," I said, and then unblushingly and in front of all those people I filched a heavy stainless steel spoon from the table and put it into my purse.

After the performance we sat in the lobby of the convention hall and discussed our reactions. One man said, "He could have had an accomplice in the audience." Another said, "The spoons might already have been weakened before he went on stage and bent them." I believed in Uri and insisted he was not doing anything fraudulent; but couldn't convince them.

As the crowd thinned out we rose and started toward the exit and there found Uri standing alone. My companions crowded around him, asking him to come to Kitt Peak and be tested under controlled conditions. I was on the outer edge of the group, but finally pushed my way forward, stuck out my hand and said, "I'm Susy Smith."

"The author?" Uri exclaimed with pleasure. "You wrote about me in a book with a blue picture of Kirlian photography on the cover."

After we talked a moment, he said, "I want to bend something for you. Have you got a key?" No key that I wanted bent out of usefulness; but as I rummaged in my purse I found the purloined teaspoon, still intact. Uri held the end of the handle with thumb and forefinger of one hand and touched the stem lightly with the first finger of his other hand. It slowly bent a tiny bit, but he gave it back to me, saying, "Conditions aren't good in here. Let's go outside," I carried the spoon close to my chest all the way; and on the front steps, completely surrounded by the skeptics, Uri held it the same way again, with thumb and forefinger, and gently stroked the top of the spoon with one finger. Right before our eyes, the teaspoon bent almost double.

As we left Uri kissed me on the cheek, and my delighted and excited companions couldn't say enough nice things to me. The next day at Kitt Peak Observatory they attempted to tell fellow workers about the amazing feat they had seen, and not one of the astronomers would even listen to them.

Yet some astronomers, as previously noted, seem to be developing open minds about such supernormal events, as have some scientists of other disciplines as well. In 1967 James had explained why they are becoming interested: "All matter can be controlled by thought, on earth and everywhere else in the universe. If I had said this to you a century ago, you would have scoffed. But now the atom has been split and found to be composed largely of space and energy. Nothing but an infinitesimal amount of matter is discovered within the preponderance of space in each tiny atom, and this infinitesimal amount of matter is described by scientists as energy, force or power."

Now he goes on to say: "This, of course, is what we in the spirit world have been attempting to convey ever since communication began. We tell you that God is the great Source of all power. We describe the basic energy, the unifying principle that permeates the universe, saying that all matter is composed of this force. Now physicists have discovered the same thing. It won't be long before all science recognizes these basic truths. Right?"

With the idea in mind of discussing the current attitude of scientists about this subject, I read and excerpted a number of library books written by today's physicists. Here are a few representative statements:

In 1981 in *A New Science of Life* Dr. Rupert Sheldrake said: "...the concept of matter has no fixed meaning; in the light of modern physics it has already been extended to include physical fields, and material particles have come to be regarded as forms of energy. The philosophy of materialism has had to be modified accordingly."

Richard Talbot in 1980's *Mysticism and the New Physics*: "There is no ultimate physical substance to matter."

Professor David Bohn of Birkback College, London, said in an interview for the Thames Television series "Mind Over Matter": "There's no sharp division between thought, emotion, and matter ... the entire ground of existence is enfolded in space."

James has indicated that he is delighted that so many men of high intellect are beginning to open their minds to new and exciting metaphysical ideas and waking up to reality. But he's not a bit happy about the mess they got us into by splitting atoms initially. And he feels that to keep on splitting them is not only bad it's frightening.

On April 27, 1979, he wrote:

"I have something to tell you. I am ready to discuss the future of your world, which is not going to last long if you keep on with atomic radiation. I have been looking into the situation carefully and it is even more dangerous than I suspected. Complete shutdown of all atomic plants and strict regulations supported by force, if necessary, to keep all the countries on earth from producing any kind of nuclear fission is imperative. I cannot be too arbitrary about this. It is of vital importance that your world knows the dangers. Joining me here are many scientists of the past who will back up what I am saying."

I wasn't about to ask him for a backup; and I can't imagine working with anyone but him or Mother anyway, so I let that go; but I asked him: "Why haven't you brought this up before when we were channeling?"

His answer: "We spirits are becoming more and more aware of the terrible dangers of any use of nuclear fission. The atmosphere is being suffused with unseen and unidentified emanations to the extent that I have to declare — atoms must not be split anywhere by anyone. The plants using nuclear fission to provide power should be closed immediately, and all tests of nuclear explosives banned. No matter how carefully buildings and reactors in which atoms are split are sealed, lowest levels of radiation cannot be kept from leaking and becoming a menace."

I had not been afraid before. I had discussed the nuclear situation as we knew it with friends, but had formed no opinions as to the danger. That's why it surprised me when James wrote so strongly about this: "Many of the world's current unexplained ailments and physical problems are caused by the radiation now in the air from all the bombs that have been and are being set off, even those underground, and also the emissions from the power plants now in use. And what are you going to do with nuclear waste? The plutonium and other residue or garbage will cause unaccountable damage when the containers in which they are disposed disintegrate.

"From our vantage point, we in the spirit world can see only trends until the event comes near enough that we are able clearly to envision the outcome. And what we initially expected has not developed. We had hoped that after setting off the bombs at Hiroshima you would never do it again. We anticipated that you would close down all installations that use nuclear fission. As it became evident you would not and that the rest of the world was also getting the know-how, we grew more and more alarmed. It is obvious that as things are now, nothing will stop your using it for energy until you invent something to take its place."

It would have been nice if he had told me about some exciting creation I could pass on to the government, but he said: "Sorry, I don't know any inventing procedures; but there are new means of finding energy which will be discovered when your technicians put their minds to it, and that should be soon. It must be soon. The problem is the emissions and refuse that you are putting into the atmosphere now. It may be impossible to retract the harm they are doing. I, and most of us here, are still confident that the human race will not erase itself from Planet Earth. But to avoid this, steps will have to be taken and taken fast."

James says all men and women have free will and that there is no big brass in the sky up above telling us how to control our lives; but "You are doing all the wrong things and this must be stopped if you wish to continue to exist. Your weakness is you let anyone do anything in the name of modern technology. You worship science rather than God. You trust your experts and their inventions to carry you blissfully into a rosy future, instead of realizing that it is your duty as individuals to take personal responsibility for keeping your surroundings ideal for living and raising your progeny. If you allow it to be completely polluted by atomic radiation, or take the chance of nuclear accidents, then you will have no decent world to leave to your descendants. And your children's children will be changed into unrecognizable mutants. It is time to start action locally, nationally and worldwide to stop all atomic experimentation and usage."

I found a clipping from *Natural History* that involves William James himself in his day on earth, and I asked him if he knew anything about it. He said, "I do remember it. It was one of my favorite stories for years." So it seems appropriate to end this chapter with it ... because James thinks too many scientists are still just like the lady in the story — convinced that their own theories are correct. And completely unwilling to be persuaded differently.

The account goes: After delivering a lecture on the solar system, philosopher-psychologist William James was approached by an elderly woman who claimed she had a theory superior to his.

"We don't live on a ball rotating around the sun," she said. "We live on a crust of earth on the back of a giant turtle."

James decided to dissuade his critic gently. "If your theory is correct, madam, what does the turtle stand on?"

"You're a clever man, Dr. James, and that is a good question, but I can answer it. The first turtle stands on the back of a second, far larger turtle."

"But what does this second turtle stand on?" James asked patiently.

The old woman crowed triumphantly. "It's no use, Dr. James — it's turtles all the way down."

CHAPTER EIGHT

EVOLUTIONARY SOUL PROGRESSION

On the subject of spiritual growth James goes like this: "When death occurs, the expectation of an abrupt alteration into some amorphous spiritual state entirely different from anything they have ever known frequently makes people unable to understand what has happened to them. For those who believe that they immediately soar into a eudaemonic heaven or dive into a fiery hell, it is a shock instead to find themselves right where they were and in what seems at first to be the identical situation."

James had trouble getting that word "eudaemonic" through me. He finally gave up and said, "Look up 'happiness' in your *Roget's Thesaurus*." I found it and then tracked it down in the dictionary and learned that it was Plato's way of discussing happiness as the main universal goal. I rejoiced that my teacher didn't use words like that very often. Although he knows them, he isn't attempting to impress with his erudite vocabulary.

"Many who die," he went on, "have already formed definite opinions as to what life will be like after passing through the portals. Fundamentalist Christians expect to be welcomed by Jesus Himself or his angels. If they find instead only relatives and friends and those spirit helpers who always attempt to greet new arrivals, they will feel neglected. If those who have preceded them were as rigid as they were in their biblical interpretations, it is likely that nothing but unhappiness has been their lot since death. They will report that no saints or angels have come to them. They'd thought befriending spirits were demons and had run away from them.

"Those who are convinced they must sleep until Resurrection Day will undoubtedly continue to sleep after death. Some who died a long time ago are still slumbering. They will eventually wake up — someone will blow a trumpet to get them up, if nothing else — and then perhaps they will listen to the truth that their physical bodies will never be resurrected but that their minds must be resurrected from misconceptions and started on the right path to development.

"Closed minds, no matter whether closed on the idea of a nebulous heaven, a long sleep in the grave, hell, nirvana, or oblivion, will get one nowhere in the spirit world. It is best to die prepared for challenging new experiences, and then whatever comes will be accepted with equanimity."

When I was a young woman lying in a cast from my hip to ankle for three months after the strep infection, a friend confided that the doctor had told her I had only one chance in a thousand to live. (This was before the days of sulpha drugs and penicillin.) Having no philosophy or religion, I was petrified at the thought of death, and from then on for years I would wake every night at midnight shaking with fright, thinking my demise was imminent. Gradually this left me, and eventually I got to the point that I didn't ponder about the ultimate future at all. Now my attitude has changed completely and I actually look forward to death. Of course, when the moment comes I don't know just how brave I'll be but tell myself there'll be no qualms. I expect a grand reunion with relatives and loved friends ... and I'll get to meet James in person.

My teacher doesn't seem to indicate that there will be too much adjustment for a person who goes over with the kind of anticipation I have. But "life after death is as individual an undertaking as life on planet earth," he says, "and you are on your own here just as much as you ever were there. If you do not listen to the enterprising spirits whose goal is to uplift their fellows, that is your business. Nobody can force you to do anything. There are no police or truant officers around here to keep you in line when you stray from accepted procedures; and there are no rulers of any kind. There are not even any rules on our plane, except the rules of courtesy, love, good will, and acceptable behavior. No one, then, can improve your character or your personality except yourself. You do not arrive at the feet of St. Peter or anyone else who will judge you, scold or applaud you, and make everything all right for you."

"With all the helpers around giving advice...." I started, but James didn't stop. "You are no more likely to listen to them after death than you were to listen to guidance on earth.

The kind of person who could never be told anything will still be that same kind of person. If you knew all the answers, you will still think so in the next life and will continue just as before until you finally realize you are getting nowhere. Then, out of pure boredom or misery, you will listen to those who state the facts and will begin to absorb their wisdom and counsel and apply it. Continuing from that point upward becomes a fascinating and enjoyable process and you will rush forward into it. Opening the mind to new ideas is difficult for most people of an obtuse nature, but once the new thoughts have been assimilated, nothing can stop the ascent."

The pace of initial advancement in the Astral depends at first on progress on earth, James tells us. It is not a matter of reward in the hereafter for good behavior or punishment for bad. It is a matter of success or failure as a person. Those who have lived a life of love and service will feel a sense of happy participation in the universal warmth almost immediately and will go forward quickly and joyously. But many who are low and miserable to begin with may remain completely oblivious to the change that has occurred. "Why, some of those who come over here in a drunken stupor may lie for ages in the gutter in which they died, even after their physical bodies have been picked up and disposed of. If they are aroused they will go right back to sleep."

That statement recalled something I needed to discuss with my mentor. "When you speak of these indigents lying in the gutters of the afterlife," I said, "it reminds me of the pathetic bums in doorways and along the streets of New York City as they were when I moved there in 1957."

I came out of my apartment building one Sunday morning and saw a dirty, ragged man asleep at the curb outside our front entrance. I commented on him to the doorman, and suggested, "You'd better call the police."

"Why?" he asked. "He hasn't done anything."

"Can't they help him? Give him a decent place to sleep?"

"They would only shake him awake and tell him to move on. If they arrested him he'd be out on the street begging again tomorrow." Since there was nothing I could do, I let it go; but I've always been very upset about this unfortunate situation in our country that is getting worse day by day. What to do about all the pain and hurt of these people? I asked James to discuss this problem, and as usual he started at another point and worked back toward the answer to my question. In the process he got around to cause and effect. He always wants us to eradicate the cause before it comes to the point of having to clean up the effect. He believes in mankind taking hold of all the evils of our existence and doing something about them.

"I do not like to preach," he wrote. "In fact, not being a preacher I do not propose to preach at this time. But I can view with alarm and I am good at that. It is time you earthlings faced up to the terrible situations in your civilization and got to work doing something about them. You people see only one side of the problem — the earth side. I see the future for these derelicts, and it is not pretty. Many of them, who die drunk or drugged, will remain like that for a long time. Dying will not wake them up and make angels out of them. They will sleep or remain in a stupor without the hope of succor or regeneration until some advanced spirit finally takes them in hand and prods them into a new existence. Think of the millions around the world who are succumbing in doped or drunken conditions. Vast numbers of us over here have to devote so much time to them, that we get little else done. Please take care of them on your side. Please, we beg you, cure them before you send them over to us. You can do it. Do not say you can't. It is just a matter of enough Samaritans caring."

"But, you know, many of these who are homeless are crazy," I observed. "Lots have been let out of mental institutions. What happens to them?"

"We have a whole brotherhood of angels who work with the mentally ill. They will attend to them immediately. What I was referring to primarily are those who are the pathetic residue of vicious habits. They need your help as much as the insane do. Stopping the drug trade by drastic measures is urgent to improve this situation. The liquor problem can be controlled also by assisting those who are addicted before they reach the point of dereliction. You need a lot more volunteers involved in AA and rescue missions. You will have to pass laws, provide and fund agencies to handle this. Spend money to clean things up."

"Yes, sir," I saluted. "I'll get on it right away." Only wishing I could. I realized the "you" he was always talking to was everyone, but I really felt like taking it personally.

James wrote more about these unfortunates. "We spirit missionaries try hard to love earthbound delinquents, but they make it so difficult. You think you have ecology problems! You certainly do. But consider ours. The atmosphere in and around and over many large cities contains an invisible crush of earthbound entities who are not willing to listen to the many spirit helpers urging them on. We must start them moving, but it is a terrible chore. That is why we are eager to get the word to you on earth so that so many will not keep coming over here to us in such a low state. Such individuals should be learning and progressing but instead are tied to former vices. They are actually dangerous because their negative attitudes can cause harm to those on earth whom they influence. Some earthbound substance users who are not quite to the point of trying to spend eternity lying in gutters but are nonetheless addicted to habitual drinking or dope, may attempt vicariously to continue to enjoy their vices by sharing those of earth addicts, urging them on to additional excesses."

I know mediums and psychics who will never go into bars under any circumstances because they can see, around many of the drinkers, spirits attempting to experience vicariously the taste of alcohol. "If such an entity finds one who overdrinks to the point of insensibility," James says, "he may quite possibly occupy the body, awaken it and have many more drinks.

"Mortals could rid themselves of addiction more easily if they knew this. Addiction, as doctors know, does not have to be permanent, and yet most of those who 'kick the habit' come right back to it because earthbounders continually influence them to resume their vices. People who are weak-willed and negative in their own personalities may be led into crime, vice, or worse — suicide. There are occasions when a person suddenly commits a crime, or even takes his own life, with no apparent possible excuse. Even someone who seems to be quite happy and without any depressing problems may commit suicide. The facts, if they were known, would usually reveal that some intruding spirit has caused the unfortunate act.

"Of course, if an obsessed individual goes to a psychiatrist, he will be treated for psychosis. Many now in institutions are there because they hear vicious voices or have strong

71

compulsions to do things they do not really want to do, as if someone else were running their lives for them. No matter how ingenuous this concept sounds, if doctors would only realize that most of these persons are, in fact, being talked to by spirits, they could be cured."

I had a curious encounter that indicates how difficult it is for a lay person to know the difference between insanity and spirit influence. I had a spare bedroom and bath in my home in Tucson and decided to rent it to bring in extra change and to give me company. A woman with a pleasant voice phoned, but when she came to see me it was revealed that she was grossly fat, perhaps 300 pounds. She wore a shoulder-length straw-colored wig that actually looked as if it were made of straw. Large dark-glasses hid her eyes, and she carried her purse in a paper shopping bag because the strap was broken. I told myself not to judge by appearances because her voice was cultured, she was clean and polite, and I needed practice on my loving-my-fellow-man exercises. So I let her pay a week's rent and move in.

Turned out she was compulsive about everything; but her compulsive cleanliness gave my kitchen a workout that perked it up considerably. She got up at 4:30 in the mornings to be dressed in time for her bus at 9:30 to go to work. (She was selling something or other on the telephone.) From 4:30 until she left the house she was busy clomping and clumping and running water, showering and washing her clothes in her bathroom sink. Also she talked aloud to herself all the time. Not an occasional phrase but a running commentary on everything.

The second day I phoned her former landlady and asked about her. I was told she was harmless. It was only her talking to herself, or someone, that was a problem. "And when she starts to yell it isn't very nice."

When she came home I informed her as kindly as possible that she'd have to leave when her week was up on Sunday because she was so noisy it spoiled my early-morning sleep. Then, still trying to help her I asked why she always wore the dark glasses, even in the house.

"My eyes aren't very pretty," she said. "I like to wear a certain brand of artificial lashes and I can't afford them right now, so I wear the glasses to hide my eyes." She told me a big hunk of her wig had fallen out in a hamburger joint and she was embarrassed. I offered to give her a nice one I'd worn during the time my hair was greying; but she refused it, saying she'd wait until she could afford a new blonde wig like the one she was wearing. She added, "It's my nose, you know. It's too big. I really should have a nose job. And I need a chin tuck." I told her, "You're just overcompensating for your weight." She replied, "Oh, yes, I'm overweight. I've gained five pounds. I'll have to go on a diet."

This was Wednesday, and about midnight after I had just fallen asleep she started talking loudly. I should say babbling up and down in baby-like cadences. Then she began screaming, "No! Don't! Stop! Get away from me!" All in that high-pitched, childish voice.

I rapped on her door and asked if she was having a nightmare. "No," she replied in normal tones, "I have a cramp in my leg. It bothers me sometimes."

Completely unnerved, I sat in the living room and read as she kept hollering and screaming and babbling intermittently the rest of the night. If she'd become really violent she could have made mincemeat of me, so I was rather uncomfortable. Panicky, actually.

The next day I spoke to the police and was told there was no way I could get her out without giving her ten days written notice unless she harmed herself or me. So for the rest of the week I took my toothbrush and nightie and slept at a friend's house around the corner.

Assuring her that she absolutely had to leave on Sunday no matter what, I said, "If you don't see an ad in the paper and worst comes to worst, you can always get a room at the YWCA."

"No," replied my eccentric guest sweetly, "I was there once and they've never let me come back again."

The story's over and I'm still intact. She called in answer to an ad in the Sunday paper and I took her there. Her new room had a private entrance and was at the far end of the house, so I didn't feel quite so bad about passing her on without a warning. No bedding was furnished, so I gave her a blanket and we parted on an up note.

Those of my friends who had seen her thought I was the crazy one for having rented to her in the first place. So did I, frankly.

I would never have dared to try to communicate with

James or Mother during that time because I was too upset and involved to be a clear channel. Now as I am writing this incident years later, I ask James about that poor woman's condition. He says: "She is not insane but her weak, neurotic character has allowed her to attract so many low spirits that there is no hope for her at this time. Were she to go to a strong medium they could be 'exorcised' but she would never do that. She has learned to live with them and accept their talking to her and disturbing her. They will leave her after her death when helpful spirits take her in hand."

James thinks "It is so easy for sophisticated moderns to toss off anything pertaining to spirit influence as balderdash because there is no scientific evidence of repeatable experiments to verify it."

I like the way Louis Richard Batzler put it in his book *The Rising Tide of Suicide*: A Guide to Prevention, Intervention and Postvention. He wrote: "Most of the skepticism and rejection of the paranormal experiences comes without investigation. Such attitudes are as unsound as blind credulity which accepts all that is taught without inquiry. Both are forms of ignorance assuming to be knowledge." Those who are the most critical have not read the literature of the field or had any personal supernormal experiences.

James goes on: "If the amount of money expended on efforts to blast men off the face of the earth were spent on attempts to prove survival, there would be enough evidence to satisfy even the most hardened skeptic. I wish it were possible to convince everyone that billions of dollars blown on weapons and on fantastic schemes of destruction could better be used to learn how to live wisely and how to die in a state of enlightenment. If the fact of survival after death was truly understood, the preservation of every individual would have value, no one would be expendable in wars, and the genuine importance of each man would be realized.

"Wars, you must know, do not kill a man; they only change him into an invisible enemy. Capital punishment does not get rid of a criminal, instead it unleashes him in an unseen form to prey on the world in a manner no less harmful.

"When Evolutionary Soul Progression is accepted, death will not be as difficult an experience as it is now for those who are unready for it. It is absolutely necessary to understand that how a person lives on earth indicates how he will exist after death, and thus it is important that each individual has a life of worth to himself and his associates. With this accomplished, he will die in a harmonious state, enabling him immediately to begin his advancement."

The griefs and tribulations of an ordinary lifetime cause much unhappiness; but, thinking about it, James says, "You will realize that it is through them that you have learned the most. How much has your temperament actually improved during the placid, uneventful periods of your life? It is the pressures you strive against that build character. Those who have only become embittered about their lot have gained little from experience, and they will have a miserable existence after death until they face up to their need for spiritual growth."

James seldom calls the earthbound "evil spirits," but I note that some of the other writers on the subject do. In 1936 in *Spiritualism's Challenge* Dr. Edwin F. Bowers wrote:

"...there is *really no such thing as an evil spirit* — in the strict sense of the term. There are low and undeveloped spirits — uneducated spirits, and who have not risen above selfish, low desires. But even these undeveloped souls are given every opportunity to rise and unfold, when rightly taught....

"No one has ever seen a *personal* God; or a devil. We have seen ignorant, sick, greedy, perverted human beings — whom we call evil — but who will in time unfold and know the truth...."

Here's another very appropriate statement, from Sir Arthur Conan Doyle in *Pheneas Speaks*. It was published in 1927. In it a spirit named Pheneas said: "Always test a spirit whether it be of God when my medium is being used. It is like taking a ticket at a gate, or else you get the riff raff in."

Pheneas was asked, "Is there much riff raff?" And he replied, "The air is thick with it. Think of the countless generations who have passed on."

"Surely they have risen?"

"Many have never tried. That is why the earth is so evil — on account of the thick cloud, the enormous aura of humans who surround the earth."

James sums up with: "Being earthbound is the worst possible thing that can happen to one. It is truly a condition of hell and is so tragic that much effort is being spent from my side to try to get the word to those on earth who are in danger of dying without any awareness of their spiritual nature.

"Life after death, when experienced properly from the onset, is so challenging and so marvelously engrossing that your present existence is nothing in comparison. But you have to keep your mind open when you arrive in order to get started off properly and save yourself much wasted time, just as you have to remain alert to new ideas and new opportunities on earth. The person with a closed mind, who will not allow any fresh concepts to enter his philosophy, will have a deplorable time after death. He will have it, that is, until he wakes up and starts his advancement. That is inevitable."

CHAPTER NINE

ONWARD AND UPWARD

"Those who envision heaven as inhabited by doddery old parties sitting around on clouds in their nightshirts strumming harps have a surprise in store," according to James. "Heaven, instead, is a place of enterprise and activity so interesting and constructive as to be a constant challenge." After death, we learn, one may begin his progression quickly, or he may stay for any length of time he chooses at the level of enlightenment where he already is. If the decision is in favor of achievement, his life immediately improves, and he is busily on his way to fulfillment.

James here gives a picture of life in the heavenly spheres if you are a progressing newcomer:

"In the first place, you look as you think you look. Because everything is controlled by thought, you appear to yourself and to others in your own mental image. Those who die young still envision themselves as youthful; but if age has withered you, as time and illness have a way of deteriorating us all, you will not wish to continue to exist as you looked when you died. So one of the first things to be done when progression starts is to think yourself rejuvenated. You will begin to feel so well without the worn-out physical body that your thoughts will reflect it; and then your appearance will take on a glow of health and happiness and youth. It is rewarding when you first meet friends over here and see that they have regained their youthful charm. It is delightful to hear that you look as well to them. Enjoyment of a body that is always healthy and vigorous is a constant pleasure. How you look is of first importance to your progression, because you could not think of yourself as old and ill and still have the positive mental attitude needed to advance."

As we've been told before, on earth with correct techniques and proper mental effort the power of thought would be able to materialize objects for us. It is the same in spirit spheres, and there is no other way for us to get anything except to visualize it. It is essential to use our thoughts properly or we will not make progress.

It just occurred to me that some readers might think perhaps I had taken *The Unobstructed Universe*, which I mentioned earlier, and used it as a model for the James material. People will invent all kinds of notions to keep from admitting that it is really possible to channel information from spirits. I'll quote a few lines from Stewart Edward White's book just to show his style ... so different from James' simple language. In line with what James has been saying above involving the use of the mind, here is White's wife Betty talking:

"Instead of our having to create clothing mechanically, for instance, we do so by a diversion of frequency. We can create directly by an impingement of our frequency on a lower degree of frequency...." (But what is this "frequency" she is talking about?) "Frequency is the essence of motion, conductivity of space, receptivity of time. But matter, as you know it — in any form — is a degree-manifestation, in time, of some *balance* between frequency and conductivity. It is no more split than is consciousness."

James' discussion goes on: "You are told by those who are instructing newcomers that you will be able to make for yourself many earth-type objects even though you have passed out of the material phase of existence. This, it is carefully explained, is because your transition will be gradual and in your earlier stages you will continue to want what you have been familiar with on earth. An abrupt alteration in your lifestyle and your customs would be difficult and disorienting. The evolutionary process is always by slow degrees.

"Thus, although sleeping, eating and drinking are nonessential, it is possible at first to indulge in them if you wish; but one learns to get along without them as time goes by." Now Susy, as a person who has always relished a good meal, an occasional Margarita, and hitting the bed at night for a great relaxing sleep, find this a bit disheartening. "It's the only thing you've said about heaven that isn't fascinating," I told James.

"It's the evolutionary system," he explained. "Eventual withdrawal from your former pursuits is essential, but it takes time. Eating and drinking are not necessary for your existence here, but at first, for one who has lived for years on strict diets, it is a great pleasure to whip up a cake or pie or cream puff and eat it with no fear of adding pounds or having a gastric attack."

"You have no idea how much I am looking forward to that," I replied enthusiastically.

He had another surprise for us. The trauma of dying does not even break the cigarette habit. But James promised the puffing did not go on for long. Well, actually, I had already read in the book *Raymond* by Sir Oliver Lodge that there were cigars in the spirit world. From my first days of research in the psychic field I remember snide references to that. This controversial book was written in 1918 by a very prominent scientist who had become convinced of life after death because he was receiving what he considered evidential communication through mediums from his son Raymond, who was killed in the First World War. There is very little in the book of a philosophical content, but in a few paragraphs Raymond attempts to tell something about what it is like where he found himself after death.

Feda, the medium Gladys Osborne Leonard's spirit control, gave a message from Raymond as follows: "He wants people to realize that it's just as natural as on the earth plane.... He says he doesn't want to eat now. But he sees some who do; he says they have to be given something which has all the appearance of an earth food. People here try to provide everything that is wanted. A chap came over the other day who would have a cigar." Feda also said, "Some want meat, some strong drink; they call for whiskey sodas."

Naturally, with no more than this to help us understand the system — Raymond had only been over a couple of months then and probably didn't know anything more by way of explanation of what he was observing — critical readers scoffed at the idea of cigars and whiskey sodas in the spirit world and dismissed the whole book as nonsense. I did, too, when I first read it. But what is said here is repeated in some of the books I read in 1979 after James' three-months writing fling.

Emily Grant Hutchings wrote in 1933 in *Where Do We Go From Here?*:

"Fred told me, in this connection, that he still ate food, but was informed that he would get over that habit in fifty years or more. Stomachs are so imbedded in all our thinking, that it is natural for us to carry them with us into the mental life, yet I had never suspected such a condition. He added that he and my brother Richard still smoked strong cigars."

Here Hutchings confirms almost exactly what James has said: "We are not 'disembodied spirits' in the sense that you mean — floating wraiths without form and substance.... When I tell you that I live in a house, and wear clothes, that I enjoy good food and good music, I want you to understand that my life here is a direct extension of the life I lived on earth."

Another who backs this up is Maurice Barbanell in *This is Spiritualism*:

"In its lowest levels people eat and drink, so long as they think it necessary to do so. They obtain the illusion, which, of course, is real to them, of what they require. And it satisfies them until they progress to higher levels where they know this kind of sustenance is unnecessary."

I hadn't realized until putting together this current book how much all James' writings have been pure Spiritualist (or spiritist, preferably) doctrine as revealed in these quotes from other books. Most of those I have read on the subject give glimpses of the same theory. James just provides a great deal of additional, more specific and detailed information.

Unfortunately, Spiritualism has been a dirty word in recent years. It was extremely popular during World War I, but since then it seems to be associated in most minds with fictitious spirit rappings and phony mediums. Today it is revived again, but mediumship is called "channeling" and the focus is much more on Eastern concepts such as reincarnation. There seems to be very little effort now to get anything in the way of proof of spirit communication, which James says is so important.

Going on about activities in the Astral plane, James says: "Whenever you wish to meet with friends, just send out a mental call to them. Some of them will surely arrive soon, ready to give you the pleasure of their company for as long as you both wish to spend in conversation. Now, when you are first in this sphere it is likely you will entertain somewhat as you did before, by feeding your guests, furnishing them with cool drinks and coffee, perhaps even liquor. Advanced visitors will humor you, although they may have grown to the point where they do not feel the necessity for such indulgences. If you had offered them nothing but your companionship, and perhaps shared with them your interesting experiences adjusting to the Astral, they would have been more than satisfied."

Just imagine a group from the same small town getting together in the home of a friend in the spirit world. Their conversation probably would not be much changed from what it was on earth, dealing largely with mutual acquaintances both here and there, but from an interestingly different point of view:

"Oh, did you know that Martha Burns is over here now?"

"Yes, I've seen her. She was ill for a long time, but you should see her now — she looks wonderful!"

"What about old Joe Sims? He's been hanging on for so long that his relations here are getting impatient."

"I know. It's sad when the spirit is so reluctant to leave the flesh. If he only knew what's in store, he would let loose and rush right on over."

"Won't you have another piece of lemon pie?" asks the hostess. "I made it myself, and, believe me, it was the most complicated cooking procedure I ever encountered. Can you believe thinking up a lemon pie? Really! Enjoy it, for it's probably the last I'll ever make."

Many old ideas and habits still hang on as we progress, James tells us. It is not until we move to more advanced planes that our thoughts will leave entirely the old ways and we will become less earth-oriented and more spirit-oriented, increasingly interested in mental and spiritual rather than physical pursuits. Then most of the remembered needs of the body fade within a relatively short while. Spiritual growth and development take care of physical needs, even to food and sex.

81

"Truly successful marriages on earth usually continue after death," James goes on. "But all marriages were by no means made in heaven. If no mental or spiritual union exists, very soon all ties are broken and each partner progresses alone. Lovers, however, may find that their emotion now has such depth and purity that it far exceeds anything in their previous experience; and often those who have not formerly had a truly good romantic involvement will find one after coming here, because spiritual love is everywhere for everyone. Even the earthbound are given our warmth and compassion, although they usually reject it. Women or men who have been childless may want to expend their loving kindness raising children, and there are recent arrivals who need nurturing and care. Remember that the spirit body is the pattern, not just a duplicate of the physical body; and so naturally the model can continue to grow without the physical organism to accompany it. So you can understand that a baby can attain adulthood in the spirit world. Some kind helper will choose to nurture and lavish attention on him, and he will grow up happily fulfilled."

In *Where Do We Go From Here?* Hutchings writes that a spirit named Isabel said: "And just because I always wanted a baby, they gave me a place in a nursery for the little children who haven't any grandmothers or aunties here to take an interest in them. It isn't a continuous job. I roam over the earth a good deal. You know, I had a terrible wanderlust, and I can indulge it to my heart's content, without worrying about the cost or bad hotel accommodations.... I am never in a hurry. I have all eternity before me to do the things I never found time for on earth." Isabel also said, "It pays to learn as much as possible about the spiritual world before you come over here."

James tells us that progressing spirits also keep busy acting as guardian angels, attempting to enlighten earthbounds, and doing "other serviceable work that allows opportunities to develop areas of growth to which they might not otherwise have been exposed. As one lives each day for others, he will soon realize that he has to think very little about his own soul's progress. He is improving himself without consciously trying."

CHAPTER TEN

GUARDIAN ANGELS

"Most people do not know they have guardian angels, but they can pretty well depend on it, especially if someone who loved them has died. He will want to stay with them a large part of the time in order to give whatever help he can." James says that "guardian angel" is a colloquial term used in the spirit world to refer to those who "as a means of self-improvement as well as a desire to assist, give their time to specific individuals on earth. There is a very definite distinction between a guardian angel, who is a newly-developing spirit, and an actual angel, who is a spirit advanced to great heights.

"When progression starts, newcomers ask more advanced spirits for advice about the steps that should be taken to develop character traits they do not have, and they will usually discover that these can be acquired by staying with earth persons who need to gain knowledge in similar areas. So they will become guardian angels for a while and give what support they can. If they are able to alleviate problems or guide their wards into wiser actions, everyone benefits, for the spirits, too, learn as they observe the learning processes of others.

"It is by our own desire that we become guardian angels," James insists, "No one forces us to do it. We actually intend to help ourselves as we help you, so do not ever feel that you are holding us against our will and keeping us from progressing by staying with you. You aid us by being object lessons for us. When we see the confusing involvements you get yourselves into, we understand how they could have been avoided, and we learn from this. By being receptive to intuition, hunches, or other 'unusual' information that comes to you, you can make use of guidance from your invisible assistants. And you can be sure that we will never force our influence on you. We do not try to make decisions for you. Another thing you can be comfortable about is that advancing spirits invariably have the good taste not to intrude themselves into your most intimate moments unless they have been especially invited."

My first indication that my mother was my guardian angel came when she told me so via automatic writing during my early efforts to communicate while living in Salt Lake City. After about nine months there, I resigned my job because Margaret, the friend I'd gone there to be with, was moving to California and I thought it would be more of a challenge to accompany her and try to live and work in L.A. So Margaret and her son and I pulled the twenty-one foot house trailer in which I was living to Santa Monica (well, my little Chevrolet Belair pulled the trailer. We went along).

Doors there seemed resolutely closed to an aspiring journalist who had no local references, so I passed my time reading all the books available in the libraries that had to do with spirit communication (not many, actually). When I learned of the research in ESP being done by Dr. J. B. Rhine's Parapsychology Laboratory at Duke University, my naive hope of finding scientific proof of immortality there was such a tremendous stimulus to me that I decided, as mentioned previously, to go there to study.

I couldn't afford the expense of having my trailer transported, so the Chevy and I, plus my little dog Junior, had to trundle it to Durham, North Carolina, by ourselves.

"You just can't do it alone, Susy," was the opinion of all my neighbors at the Santa Monica trailer court. None of the women would have dreamed of attempting it, they said. Hands were thrown into the air in horror — all because I was planning to drive my car across the United States by myself with a trailer in tow. One man was frank enough to say, "I wouldn't even try to pull a trailer that far alone myself, and I don't have the physical handicap you do."

A friend said, "I couldn't possibly do such a thing. I'd be scared to death."

"Well, do you think I'm not?" I asked her.

Still, I had this compulsion to learn more about the psychic field from professors, and at that time the Parapsychology Lab at Duke was the only place to go. So I had to take a chance on this lonely trip.

Anyway, I was beginning to suspect that I would not be alone. Since Mother had said she was my guardian angel I'd had one or two bits of evidence that maybe she really was trying to assist me from time to time: such as moral support when I attempted to paint my trailer turquoise and ended up with a really professional-looking job. Also I had a dream shortly before leaving that encouraged me to believe her help would be available.

In the dream I was driving my car in West Texas and Mother was sitting beside me. There was a lot of water on the highway, and we were aware that there had been big storms in the area. Water was soon crowding the car, ominous cliffs closed in on us, and there were great dark clouds overhead. I was frightened. Then Mother told me to move over and let her drive. As she took the wheel the cliffs immediately began to recede and the sun came out. Then the road ahead became a placid lake, the car turned into a boat, and we sailed right over the water.

I awoke at 6 A.M. and lay in bed trying to interpret the dream. Obviously it meant that I should put myself into Mother's hands so she could pilot me and then everything would be all right. I reached out as usual and turned on the bedside radio, and the newscaster was saying, "Last night a sudden storm hit West Texas and floods occurred in many areas."

After I started off on my trip east I discovered that pulling a trailer alone is at best slightly nerve-wracking, and so is Los Angeles traffic. Putting them both together makes an excellent excuse for staying home and crawling under the bed.

I made it to Indio the first night and drew into a mobile home court of sorts where there was no one to help me get installed, so I had to do without lights, water, plumbing, and other accoutrements of refined living. Also I had to back my own vehicles into a plot, something I'd never done before. Once when I managed to jam the back bumper of the car tightly against the gas tanks on the front of the trailer, there was a screeching as if the car had run over the six tails of six cats. But finding nothing damaged, I resumed operations, eventually landing my home-on-wheels in a space sufficiently out of the way that it could remain there overnight.

It was dark and sharply cold by then, and I sought refuge inside, tired out and freezing. Dinner by flashlight was a cold meatloaf sandwich accompanied by a fine, dry, distinguished California root beer, served lukewarm. And so to bed, with my clothes on and my dog curled closely against my stomach for warmth. This was not quite the Beverly Hilton.

At six the next morning, as I was leaving, my glance just happened to fall on a piece of bolt on the ground in front of the car. It was turquoise and undoubtedly off my trailer, but where? I finally discovered that the gas tanks were loose and realized that backing the night before had sheared off the bolt which secured them to the frame. If my eyes hadn't strayed onto the tiny object on the ground, my tanks might have bounced off in transit.

Not knowing where to have such damage repaired, I stopped at the first business establishment that was open along the highway — a lumber yard. There a boy put a new bolt on in five minutes and wouldn't charge me for it. By then I was beginning to wonder if something more than coincidence might not be involved in such good luck.

A few nights later I was in Ozona, Texas, and the next morning as I left there was a heavy fog. The hazy driving didn't bother me particularly, for I rather hoped that my unseen mother was out ahead blazing the trail. But as the sun glared forth about 9 o'clock and we picked up speed over the hills, persistent ideas started bombarding me to pull over to the side of the road and stop.

I said to myself, "Better get my sun glasses out of the glove compartment" and answered, "No, wait until the first roadside park." Because there was also a handbrake to manipulate in order to slow the trailer, as well as the controls of the car to operate, it was too much effort just to pause alongside the road; and I couldn't reach the glove compartment without stopping. Next I thought, "Really should get out some eye drops. They'll make me more alert." And decided again to wait until the next turnout. Right on top of this came the thought that maybe it would be wise to make sure the new bolt was still holding the gas tanks on safely. It all seemed silly, yet the impressions to stop were so insistent that I finally pulled over. As the trailer bumped to an unusually jerky halt I reflected on the dangers of roadside gravel, vowing never to stop on it again.

Going back to check on the gas tanks, just in case, I found that the connection which plugged the trailer brake into the car electric outlet was unhitched and the socket was dragging on the ground! Its prongs were becoming so bent that another few feet of travel would probably have finished their usefulness. Had I tried to go down a hill, of which there were many on that highway, or to stop suddenly without the brake functioning, the trailer, as well as the car and its occupants, would all have made a spectacular splash in the nearest ditch.

"Thank you, Mother," I said with the most fervent conviction yet exhibited. A few more incidents like this and I was going to be firmly dedicated to the principle of guardian angels. There were several other indications on that trip, and since then there have been many more throughout my life.

Actually, it appears that I have two guardian angels, one, so to speak, by default. When my mother died and didn't need his protection any longer, her grandfather was passed on to me. How I learned about him is kind of neat. After I settled down in Daytona Beach, my next stop after the Parapsychology Laboratory, I started going to the local mediums to see if anyone could give me evidence of survival. One lady provided only a brief message — that an older man with a beard was with me who looked like me from the nose up. She added, "He's related to you. You have a picture of him at home." The only picture I had of an older male relative with a beard was of my great-grandfather. I guess you could say there's a family resemblance in the wave of his red hair, which was just like Mother's, and I looked kind of like her.

When I arrived home I took my pencil in hand (we hadn't graduated to the typewriter at that time) to attempt a chat with Mother to question her about Grandpa. I asked who the medium had been describing, and the pencil wrote, "Your great-grandfather." Then it scrawled very forcibly, "Anderson."

"Who's writing?" I asked.

"I'm your mother's grandfather."

"Was it you the medium saw tonight?"

"It was."

"Can you identify yourself further?"

"I am Robert Ingram Anderson."

"Where did you live?"

"Oakland, Maryland."

"Is it really you?" I asked, still needing assurance.

"I'm really Grandpa."

I finally greeted him warmly, and he wrote a bit more that is not of consequence here, and that is the last time I've been in touch with him. I certainly had no inkling he was my guardian angel or even that he had continued to remain with me until James revealed it in 1979. The way James told me about Grandpa was in the following script:

"More and more people are becoming aware of the need for help from their guardian angels or other spirit associates and are eager to start communicating with them. It is unwise unless they have learned how to protect themselves thoroughly. Many have written Susy asking how to be sure who their guardian angels are. It is probably a loved one who has died, and that is really enough for them to know. However, if no one near has passed over, it could easily be a grandparent, or even a great-grandparent, as in Susy's case."

James shifted gears now as he often does and started addressing the reader directly: "It is only necessary to know that your guardian angel is someone who loves you or who is interested in you in some way, and when you turn to him in times of trouble you will receive the best positive thoughts he is able to send you. His help is of much more value when you ask for it and accept it joyfully."

I had let James keep running on here because he was on a roll; but when he paused I said, "What do you mean, 'a great-grandfather as in Susy's case'?"

James continued writing to the reader instead of answering me directly, but what he said was of special interest because I hadn't known Grandpa was my G.A.

"It was Susy's mother's grandfather who always guarded and loved her mother, Betty, through her life on earth and then turned his watchfulness to Susy when Betty joined him in the spirit world. Susy learned of his presence through a medium and then by automatic writing with him. An ancestor could be your guardian angel.

"If you have no relative on the other side who might be particularly interested in you, perhaps someone who is not related to you has become your guardian angel because of mutual interests. If you have a special talent, or if you enjoy a specific hobby, perhaps this has struck a responsive note in someone in the spirit world. You can just about depend on it that most of the good things that have happened to you have been helped along by some kind of angelic assistance."

The way to let guardian angels work for us, I have learned, is by being receptive to the thoughts they project to us, as Mother sent me those insistent messages to stop the car on the West Texas hills.

James went on with, "The idea that one could possibly be receiving assistance from an unseen entity might seem repulsive to some people who like to think of themselves as the captains of their ships, the masters of their souls. A spirit guide operating constructively on their behalf will take nothing away from their own development, and can add immeasurably to it, but they would never want to admit this. I am sure that those with this attitude will always be reluctant to consider that 'spooks' had anything to do with them."

"You shock me," I remarked amiably, "using such a derogatory word."

"I was just revealing the way that many independent individuals think. Now let me tell you how a spirit who is beginning his progression and decides he can best improve himself by aiding others goes about it. He reevaluates his own situation first. One of his initial exciting discoveries in the Astral plane is that all his memories are intact and available to him. If he wishes to remember any moment of his life, it is there in all detail. For a while he may have fun recalling persons and places he has not thought of in years. He soon becomes aware that this can cause real anguish, however, as he allows himself to relive some of his most traumatic experiences. So he stops the self-torture. But when he begins really to work on his progression, it will be necessary for him to make a systematic survey of his life, going into all his memories carefully to learn where he made mistakes and recalling all the occasions when he did less than his best. Many unhappy events will have to be reviewed in detail so that he can learn how to make amends."

For many nights during the past decade I underwent something strange and unwanted around three or four A.M. I would wake up and lie for an hour or two with disturbingly unpleasant scenes of my entire life running through my mind.

89

Now I've done a lot of kookie things in my past, but I always meant well. Like most people, probably, I have never consciously done a malicious thing at any time; and so my nightly repetitive reviews were not of bad or unkind incidents. They were instead reminders of the many dumb things I've done, or perhaps times when I made what I thought were bright remarks that were taken wrong and possibly hurt someone. I've also had a few unsuccessful romances. Nothing I'd want to keep going over in my mind some forty or fifty years later, for heaven's sake. But apparently my soul was cleaning house and wanting me to go into each incident in great detail. It was grueling.

Finally it dawned on me that there must be a purpose in all this. I began deliberately to forgive the people involved in each of these dismal memories, and then to forgive myself; and after I ran through the entire list, they began disappearing. I hated going over past mistakes, but now, at least, I've done it. I hope it won't be necessary to go through this whole rigamarole again on the other side.

James says a spirit enduring this is now "in a position to see the reasons for many of the errors he made, even those early in life. Some of them can be rectified by thinking them through from a constructive point of view and understanding all the situations involved. Others may have been so unfortunate that more will have to be done in order to correct them. Yet each incident of his life will have to be mentally reviewed with the object of making amends for anything that requires it. In many cases he may, even at this late date, be able to alter the situation for the better by his proper thinking and corrective mental application."

James gives an example of how a newly-developing spirit goes about remaking himself in one particular aspect of his character. Supposing that in reviewing his life a great many prejudices of a very deep-seated nature are discovered. "He may have taken adequate care of his family and died thinking that in general he was a relatively decent sort of chap," James writes. "Proper reconnaisance of his life now, however, reveals that there is one entire area in which there was a complete blind spot. He had racial prejudice. Therefore, no matter how tolerant he believed himself to have been, there is a tremendous amount to learn. When it was impossible for him to think of a black as anything but an inferior person, he

90

himself was inferior. Now that he faces the fact that he went through life on earth with a distorted image of the truth, he will have to decide how to correct it."

James says that any teacher to whom this prejudiced white spirit goes for advice will tell him, "Until you can feel equally at home with anyone who is black or white or yellow or red or any beautiful tint in between, you will not have learned brotherly love." So he will probably decide that the best form of growth is to go to live in the terrestrial home of an underprivileged black man and act the role of guardian angel for him and his family. From the vantage point of invisibility, he will be able to observe everything that happens to them and be aware of what each is thinking. Soon he will begin to know what it means to have different skin color in a predominantly white civilization.

The idea is that the white spirit lives with this black family during the day, and at night he spends his time at art classes and playing bridge and improving his mind and helping others and doing all those pleasant other-world things. In his state of timelessness he is able to live with these people for years and watch the kids grow up. By sending positive thoughts and sound advice he helps them through all kinds of problems. "He will undoubtedly become fond of the children," James says. "It is not possible to look into the mind of a child and not learn to love him. Soon he will have genuine knowledge of what it means to walk in the shoes of another. Will it then be possible to feel superior to any race?"

We have another example: Say a developing spirit has been intolerant of alcoholics. Instead of realizing an acquaintance who drank too much was sick, he scorned him and spoke disparagingly of him. After self-evaluation, he admits the necessity to learn compassion and so he chooses to assist this drinker as part of a campaign for mutual improvement. In this man's home, reading his mind, it is easy for the guardian angel to understand the terrible humiliation the alcoholic undergoes each time he comes out of a drinking episode, the intolerable hardship it is for him to realize what he is doing to his family. The spirit is aware of the arguments this man has within his soul before he succumbs once again to his desire for liquor; and he observes the earthbounds hanging around urging him on. By talking to the latter and convincing them to leave, the spirit's time will have been well spent for everyone concerned. And perhaps his invisible encouragement will be enough to get the drinker started with Alcoholics Anonymous. As for this guardian angel's reaction — understanding fully the problems of this man will have helped him grow in wisdom and undoubtedly will have cured his intolerance.

In a book called *The Ministry of Angels* Joy Snell says that "guardian angels have fought life's battles bravely and conquered ... and thereby they gained the knowledge, experience and wisdom which fits them to be ministering angels to those who are passing through trials and temptations similar to the trials and temptations which beset themselves in their earthly careers." They minister to us by striving to impress us with thoughts of patience, of courage, of God. "Often, very often, they fail, for often, alas, the minds of those they strive to influence are too darkened by gloomy, selfish, or debasing thoughts to admit the light the angels would bring them.... If people could only be made to realize that there are guardian angels watching over them, ever eager and anxious to help them to resist temptation, to conquer selfishness, to develop their spiritual natures, to seek abiding peace where it alone can be found, they would avail themselves of this God-sent help. Then humanity would not long present the sad spectacle it now does."

CHAPTER ELEVEN

THE HEAVENLY HIERARCHY

"Yes, angels and gods really do exist," says James. "They are people, just as you and I, but people in the tremendously advanced stages of near perfection and actual perfection. It should be inspiring to you to realize that you, too, will someday reach such an exalted peak in your development. Everyone will. Angels are highly-advanced spirits, and gods are angels who have improved themselves to the point of personal achievement where they are actually aware at all times of their great and wonderful union with Ultimate Perfection."

"You have me believing in them," I said, "but aren't the terms awfully quaint for this ultra-modern world?"

"Perhaps, but they are the familiar words we here use for the higher states. Let us have our few idiosyncracies, most of the time we are fairly sophisticated."

I was pleased to find that my teacher was sustained in this by Dr. Gina Cerminara's book *Insights for the Age of Aquarius*. Gina was a friend of mine, a highly educated woman whose *Insights* is one of the cleverest books I've ever read. In a chapter titled "Hierarchy, Angels and Gods," she says that it is a very large assumption "To assume that God is directly above ourselves, with no intermediate intelligences in between ... and that any seemingly strange or supernatural phenomena must necessarily have been produced by the Supreme Godhead of all the Universe."

"On our planet there are thousands of different kinds of creatures, from tiny one-celled forms on up," Gina points out. "So why," she asks, "should man be the highest point of development? Wouldn't it be more logical to assume that the sequence continues beyond man, in a hierarchy of form, intelligence, and consciousness that may not be visible to man but nonetheless real?"

It encouraged me to see what good support Gina gives to the theory of angels and gods. No matter how naive it may appear to modern readers, the ideas are sensible, she main-

93

tains, for wherever we see a successfully functioning organization — the army, governments, big business, large churches, universities — we see a hierarchial system in operation: people in graded ranks with authority delegated to them from higher levels in the scale. It is logical, then, to infer that a similar hierarchy could exist for the running of the vast organization which we call the universe.

Gina says, "Modern educated persons usually regard angels and gods as a superstitious relic of ignorant ages, but perhaps the whole idea deserves to be re-examined."

Another who backs up this theory is Israel Regardie, who in *The Tree of Life* speaks of: "... a certain hierarchy of gods, each having a specific task in the evolution and governance of the universe."

As to where these advanced souls come from, we have no less an authority than Jesus Christ, who is recorded in Matthew, Chapter 18: "Jesus called a little child to him and set him in the midst of them and said (18:10) 'Take heed that ye despise not one of these little ones; for I say unto you, that in heaven their angels do always behold the face of my Father which is in heaven.'" As this is translated, how can it mean anything other than that the child becomes an angel and eventually sees God?

Again we come to modern science. An article titled "Cosmic Interaction" by British Telecommunications Engineer Edgar A. Tooke says: "It is by no means uncommon now for physicists to postulate a universal consciousness.... A theory is gaining ground, however, among biologists which strongly infers the activity of conscious entities controlling the evolutionary processes." Which is exactly what James' gods are up to.

"Life would never be endurable for long periods unless one had constructive work to do," James tells us. "At the highest level gods' occupations consist of such activity as forming new galaxies or inventing an original type of insect or animal for an already existing but newly developing planet. Think of the joy it must be to dream up some novel creature that is going to be reproduced in matter and live in a physical body in some new world!"

"You mean," I interrupted, "we have *them* to thank for mosquitos and flies?"

"Afraid so, in an indirect way."

"Now what does that mean?"

"It means that the evolutionary process sometimes takes species in different directions from the original blueprint. Variations are allowed for by the system, but some are not as successful as others."

Then he went on: "This explanation of origins should not seem too preposterous to those whose thinking has advanced beyond the idea that everything happens by chance or by natural selection starting from some unknown source. And certainly no one who is reading these words still believes that an anthropomorphic god with a long white beard accomplished it all with a wave of his hand. So how do you suppose everything gets done? By the conscious thoughts and inventions of those expert aspects of Ultimate Perfection known as gods.

"All the animals, trees, flowers, insects ... all life of every kind that exists on our planet was originally consciously devised by highly developed spirits who came here from other planets. In many instances the evolutionary process has then taken effect to modify the originals into the species you now see. It is a great challenge to put new organisms into existence on a spinning ball of dirt when it has attained the proper conditions so that life can be sustained."

As I was copying the DeWitt Miller paragraph quoted in chapter three, I questioned Miller's concept of man's evolution. "If man was designed by gods, he certainly didn't come all the way up through time from amoebas, did he?" I asked my mentor.

"No," he replied. "When the planet was judged ready for intelligent human life, various attempts were made by gods to develop from available organisms bodies with opposable thumbs that could walk erect and thrive under earth conditions. Several different prototypes were designed, but they did not prove satisfactory. It was not until the earliest prehistoric man was produced and found to be capable of living successfully on earth that a soul (or conscious awareness of self) was placed within his body. From then on he evolved in a gradual pattern of growth to his present state.

"As man progressed physically from his earliest beginnings, so he is also progressing spiritually, but at what sometimes seems to be a snail's pace rather than a human's."

James points out that sexual delineations continue into the angel and god states. "Male and female retain their identities as such, but not for amatory reasons. Sexuality applies to mortality only for the uses of reproduction on earth. But the distinction between the sexes is important throughout time, for there must be the two opposites which will complement each other.

"As they progress it is necessary for those who have been sexually confused on earth to reassess their natures and to decide which sex they wish to remain forever. When they make up their minds, then think of themselves definitely and firmly as their chosen sex, that is what they become permanently. They have to be one or the other; there are no homosexuals in advanced stages of spiritual development. Although some perfectly normal males have female characteristics and vice versa, there is nonetheless a distinction. It is important to keep the two sexes separated so that there will ultimately be male gods and female gods, with their diverse essential qualities delineated. And the two are never blended into one that is asexual or bisexual. Anything you may have heard or read to the contrary is wrong."

The very fact that everything follows a system reveals, James says, that "the universe is not a chaotic mess of unorganized exploding stars and matter going hither and thither without direction. It is managed and coordinated in its every action by gods. Everything revolves around the inhabited planets, because the production of humans and their advancement to the god state and return in a perfected condition to Ultimate Perfection is the purpose of it all.

"While gods are doing all this enterprising creating in outer space, among their many other inspirational duties," says James, "angels spend most of their time assisting mortals and earthbound spirits. When what seems to you to be a miracle occurs, expect an angel to be back of it.

"When we on our plane see angels, it is as great glowing lights; but they have progressed so far and they pulsate at such a high frequency that we are unable to see them most of the time. It takes effort for them to reduce their vibrations to the point that their presence can be observed by us. It is even more difficult for them to make themselves visible to you on earth, and that is one of the reasons angels are so seldom on view. On the rare occasions when this occurs, the angel's frequency has to be lowered to earth's density in order to be seen by a mortal.

"Angels want to be regarded as loving brothers and sisters who ask you to appeal to them in time of trouble or need. Although it is an essential to human development that there be trials and tribulations as growth processes, when it is something you can't handle alone, they want to help you. So petition the angels whenever you are in bad trouble of any kind, and then make yourself receptive to their assistance. They will come, although you probably will not be able to see them."

"If angels and gods do all the God work, what role does Ultimate Perfection play in all this?" I asked.

"The entire role."

"I'm afraid I don't understand."

"He performs through the action of His units of operation — the gods. Each god is so much a part of the whole that every universal thought includes him. Gods are aware at every moment of their unity with Ultimate Perfection. That is why they can knowingly do His will."

"If we are of such personal concern to God," I said, "the logical question now is 'why does he allow tragedies and terrible calamities to occur?'"

"It is understandable to wonder about this," was the answer. "But nothing that occurs is deliberately planned or foreordained, and everyone has free will. The law of cause and effect is in operation at all times and when certain steps are taken or negatives are thought, specific results are created. It is inevitable that mischances occur and sometimes they are devastating. But what happens, even when it is sadly disheartening, is not consequential in the long run, as I am sure you have already grasped by now. What is of consequence is what is gained from it by the people involved.

"All the gods and angels are aware that whatever you can learn now you will not have to learn in the spirit world. Their view of your ultimate destiny is as comprehensive as your view would be of the human growth potential of your baby. Thus gods and angels do not become anguished over any tragic circumstance that occurs in your life any more than you would cry if your baby stubs his toe. They understand its relationship to your overall long-term life experience just as you are aware of the insignificance of a tiny tripping.

"It is to angels that we must eventually look," we are told, "to solve the problem of some earthbound spirits who have been in their desperate straits much too long. After having ignored all succor from those missionaries who spend hours and days and even years endeavoring to pick them up and put them on their feet, there comes a time when they are ultimately turned over to the angels. No matter how depraved a spirit might be, when he sees a vision of glowing light and beauty who gives him an inspirational talk, he will listen. For this reason I am able to state that no soul is ever lost for all time. Ultimate Perfection will not allow any part of Himself to be thrown away permanently. He wants it all back."

One of the greatest mediums who ever lived was Andrew Jackson Davis, and he wrote several books by automatic writing when he was in a trance state. In *The Penetralia* (1858) he proposed this question: "Did God elect some to everlasting life, and others to endless destruction?" His answer was: "God is the Father of the spirits of all men. Hence all men *have their entire existence* in the one omnipresent Spirit of Deity. Think you that the Whole can be happy when many of its *parts* are miserable? Human souls are detached individualized personifications of the Deific Nature and Essence; and the imperfection or destruction of a single detachment would, like the loss of a wheel from a perfect watch, impair the goodness and derange the infinite precision of the Universal Mechanism."

James says that eventually some angel will be able to convert the earthbound entity from his degraded ways to start him on the right path. None is so corrupt that an actual visitation by a shining eminence will not straighten him out and head him in the proper direction. But if angels went after every earthbound spirit before everything else that can possibly be done is tried, they would have no time to accomplish anything else.

About our need for help here on good old Planet Earth, James has this to say: "Personally, if I were living on earth at the present time and knew what I now know, I would be calling on the angels constantly. I would start clubs and organizations all over the world for the purpose of involving as many people as possible in a great campaign of prayer for assistance. You are at a very low point right now in your history because there are so many formidable things going on.

"We have not given up on you, though. We know what the destiny of earth should be, and it is great. With your clever technology and your awakening widespread interest in your fellow men, you should eventually come out all right. But at present conditions for almost everyone in every area of the planet are so negative and you are in such a low spiritual slump that you must do something about it. The best advice I can possibly give you is to begin your positive thinking on a massive scale, work hard to convince everyone how important it is, and ... call the angels!"

CHAPTER TWELVE

MEDIUMS, CHANNELERS, WHATEVER

In a world that doesn't know about calling angels for help or how to protect itself from evil spirits, we're obviously just muddling through. We're ignoring everything supernormal that might affect our lives and thus living with only part of the knowledge necessary to contend adequately with existence. This I have on good authority. If we took mediums seriously instead of making fun of them, we could soon gain information about the unknown that would help open up important aspects of life. James tells us: "To find a good medium of communication is a wonderful accomplishment for us. So many on this side are eager to get the word about life after death through to the world, and psychics are one of our few options. If certain mediumistic or strongly psychic persons were subsidized by governmental or other funds so that most of their hours could be given to developing their abilities to communicate, and if these were properly supervised by technicians with an intelligent appreciation of what they were doing, proof of survival after death could be achieved within a few years' time.

"Today it is too easy for individuals who have some slight psychic ability to make a reputation and money by occasional minor feats of clairvoyance, telepathy, precognition or healing, or by giving past life readings. Unfortunately, very few will go to the trouble of developing their capacities to the point where they can receive accurate spirit communication."

James points out that going into deep trance is almost a lost art today. It is too much trouble to learn and too uncomfortable to endure; and so even those who could develop powerful mediumship of this sort do not bother.

"The great trance mediums I have researched and written about all disliked this technique intensely," I said. "It's hard to blame them, for they always had to miss all the enjoyment of their séances."

"Yes, when asleep they are unable to participate in the activities, and they learn about what occurred only when they come out of trance."

"Imagine entertaining a former president or some famous historical personage while you are asleep and just being told about it afterward. That's no darn fun."

"Fortunately, however," James said, "deep trance is not necessary in most cases for the information we wish to impart. It is possible for us to get accurate messages through a medium who is mildly entranced. So this is what we wish to encourage among psychic folk today.

"When the time comes that such ability is looked on as a great talent and mediums are taken seriously by the general public, then more will spend time and effort to develop. In my day people stayed at home in family groups, and it was not so difficult for training classes to be formed. Now everyone is always too busy. Or they are watching television. I do not know when your customs will change again to a simpler mode, but until then spirits like me are crying in the wilderness for those who will become involved in this particular type of growth."

James continues: "I am not necessarily recommending that psychics go into professional mediumship, for talents fluctuate, and if one is making his living by his supernormal abilities and is incapable of performance on occasion, it is almost traumatizing. If he is unable to produce genuine phenomena or messages, he should be obligated to return the sitter's money; yet if his livelihood depends on it, he is too often tempted to fill in with the fruits of his imagination ... or even, in some cases, fraud."

It may not be easy at first for one who wishes to find a meditation or development class, we are told, and no one should attempt to learn mediumship without the support of a group or a "sensitive" (psychic) whose guides or protective forces are established. In other words, sitting for development alone is not recommended. But people willing to spend time together attempting psychical growth attract spirits who give their support and assistance in an effort to help one or more of the group progress mediumistically. They will ward off any intruders who might attempt to disrupt the activities. All sitters will grow spiritually when they gather together, even though there may not be results of a psychical nature for

101

quite a while. This is because, James tells us graciously, "We bring you great measures of love, and we are always willing to work endlessly for your advancement. You will feel this loving warmth to the point that you will come to look forward to your weekly class nights with anticipation."

During most of the '70s an ESP development class met at my home one night every week. Once, while we were taking a break, a member who has occasional remarkable spontaneous psychic experiences went out on the porch for a cigarette fix. When she returned she was startled to see the entire living room filled with hazy gray swirls. It briefly crossed her mind that perhaps the non-smokers inside had all puffed clouds of smoke to shame her. That thought was replaced immediately by the realization that what she was seeing was a room full of spirits, who gradually took more distinct shapes. She says she couldn't help but be indignant that the rest of us should all be gaily chatting about mundane things in the presence of so many supernatural beings; but even after she told us that we had guests, none of us was able to see them.

Physical mediumship is seldom found today in this country, and we don't hear much about it; but James is all for it. He says that if certain psychically gifted persons were sponsored and subsidized so that they could afford to spend large amounts of their time developing an ability for physical mediumship, it would be of great help to the spirits in their efforts to communicate. When asked why physical mediumship is of value as a means of proving survival, he tells us:

"Physical energy, or psycho-kinetic force, is produced in the bodies and from the minds of some humans more than others. When we spirits find persons with these innate qualities and capabilities, we wish to encourage them to build up this power as much as possible. It is then available for us to use in our manifestations. It is true that our helping a physical medium to bend teaspoons does not prove survival. However, if this ability were used in other directions, it could supply proof. Here are the lines along which initial research should be instigated and encouraged:

"1. Attempts to receive fingerprints of deceased persons whose prints are already on record. If there is a strong medium and carefully-controlled conditions, there is no reason this should not be success-ful.

"2. There are numerous attempts going on today throughout the world to receive voices of spirits on tape recorders and radios and their faces on television screens. The conditions are not perfected, and projection from our end as well as reception from yours is extremely difficult at the present time. But with a scientific approach to the problems entailed, the time will come when good reception is possible. The goal, of course, is to perfect the techniques so that voices and faces of the deceased can be received and compared with voice prints and pictures they left on earth. Today the most successful work with electronic communication is being done in Europe, and results are quite encouraging.

"3. Spirit photography has occurred frequently but has almost always been questioned as fraud, whether rightfully so or not. When enough strong physical mediums are working on this with Polaroid cameras under controlled conditions, results will be spectacular."

When effort in any of these three areas is implemented, it will be possible to obtain proof of life after death, according to our teacher. "Do not be discouraged if it does not come quickly," he says. "With sufficient effort it will come."

A good medium, we are told, is of great help in discouraging earthbound entities from causing trouble. Mediums are often able to speak to these intruders and wake them to the truth of their situation; so no mental institution should be without the services of one for consultation. Long ago Dr. Carl Wickland, who was the head of an asylum, discovered that his wife was a medium. He wrote in *Thirty Years Among the Dead* (published in 1924) how, with her help, he was able to remove a number of entities who were possessing some of his patients. The patients were given shock treatment to dislodge the spirit intruders, who were then conducted by spirit helpers from their victims into the entranced medium's body. They spoke through her, told who they were, and usually indicated that they were in a very disorganized mental state. Dr. Wickland talked to them, telling them what had actually happened to them, and instructed them not to return to the victim but to start their progression instead.

One of Dr. Wickland's cases involved a little boy named Jack T. of Chicago, who'd had a good disposition until, at the age of five, he began to act and think like an adult, and have an uncontrollable temper. He was a good-looking child, but now he talked constantly of being old and ugly; and he was so intractable that efforts to correct him proved of no avail, so his parents asked Wickland for help. Then a spirit whose actions and expressions were in every way like those the boy had been exhibiting spoke through Mrs. Wickland and explained his situation.

"This entity," wrote Dr. Wickland, "said his name was Charlie Herrmann; he was aware of having died and declared that he was a very homely man, with ugly features and a face covered with pockmarks. Nobody cared for him and this fact preyed on his mind.

"Someone had once told him that after death individuals could reincarnate and become whatever they wished to be. Since his only desire was to be good looking, so that others would not shun him, he decided to try to reincarnate.

"As a result, he became entangled in the magnetic aura of a small boy and was unable to free himself."

Finding himself helplessly imprisoned and unable to make anyone realize it, Charlie Herrmann had outbursts of temper and "felt like flying to pieces," he said. They called him Jack and he didn't like it. He had been miserable while attached to the child but could do nothing about it. Through the help he received from the Wicklands, he was freed, and very grateful; and Jack became the good and happy boy he had been previously.

I hope the spirits who took Charlie off taught him right away how to think himself handsome.

Some Spiritualist churches have rescue circles in which the medium goes into trance as Mrs. Wickland did and low entities are allowed to speak through him/her. "When earthbound spirits converse with the members of the circle," James says, "and are told the truth about their condition, they will listen, because their attention is so centered on earth that they can see and hear humans more readily than they can those of us on their own side of life. If you people once reach their ears with the truth, then they are more likely to hear us when we try to assist them. And so a medium should always start talking to unenlightened spirits any time he sees one or senses his presence. I believe the time will come when psychics will feel this to be one of the obligations imposed on them by their unusual talents. Theirs is a great endowment and one not to be taken lightly.

"Mediums would be of special value to doctors who work with mental patients, if they were employed. But with medical understanding such as it is today, it seldom happens that intruding spirits are recognized and eliminated. When a psychiatrist or psychologist is able to bring himself to use the services of a psychic, he finds that many of his patients are revealed to suffer from the influence of earthbound entities."

An incident told me by my friend Dr. Russell MacRobert, the late New York City psychologist, neurologist and psychical researcher, involved a patient of his and the medium Frank Decker. In the years before they both died the doctor and the medium had developed a mutually advantageous arrangement whereby Decker occasionally assisted with suggestions about patients. The following is an example of how the services of a medium can be of value to a psychiatrist:

One day Decker dropped by the doctor's Park Avenue office and remained until MacRobert had time to see him. A young man also sitting in the waiting room particularly interested the medium and he watched him carefully. After the patient had seen the doctor and gone, Frank Decker went in. He asked immediately, "Who was that young man who just left?"

"Why?" countered the doctor, sure that something interesting was coming.

"Because he has a real bad problem," said Decker. "There's a dirty old man with him, hanging around so closely that he is almost overshadowing the patient's personality."

"What does he look like?" MacRobert asked.

Unhesitatingly Decker said, "He's toothless, and he's very unenlightened. He does not even know he is dead. He seems to be clinging to the young man as one in a dream, not really knowing what's going on."

Dr. MacRobert later told me how helpful this information was in his analysis of the patient. "That boy," he explained, "was less than thirty but he had a strange fixation about being old. It was all I could do to convince him that he should not go and have all his teeth pulled out. He thought of himself as prematurely aging, tired, ill, and with decayed teeth — although anyone who looked at him could see that he was in excellent shape, and so were his teeth. I'd had great difficulty with him, not knowing his actual problem. When Decker saw the toothless old man possessing, or at least obsessing him, I knew what to do."

I'm going with the flow these days and calling myself a channeler. I never liked using the word "medium," and "psychic" and "sensitive" are a little too vague. "Channelers" is the currently accepted name for people who purport to provide messages from spirits, although few of them seem to be spending much time today attempting to bring evidence of life after death.

Alan Vaughn, a most successful medium whose precognition of the future has now made him famous as a "psychic predictor" (another new term for old-timers like James and me), teaches channeling classes and writes books about the subject. He says in an article in *New Realities*, Jan./Feb. 1987:

"Could it be part of our spiritual evolution that an increasing number of people are attempting to make contact with higher consciousnesses? For many, the experience of channeling is uplifting and gives life meaning. It creates a spiritual context that may be lacking in traditional religions. Since the subject of channeling is to make direct contact with higher beings, whereas in traditional religions one just reads about them, the thrill, the immediacy of that contact with higher consciousnesses, may be the driving force behind the phenomenal growth of the practice of channeling."

Later Alan explains what channelers do:

"The prevalent style of channeling today is bringing through philosophical messages — messages designed to help people think. This style can be effective in evoking positive changes in outlook and lifestyle, but there is seldom any hint of ESP at work. Indeed, attempts by some psychical researchers to test the validity of a channeler by asking ESP-type questions (What will the temperature be tomorrow in Seattle?) are not only ludicrous, but quite beside the point. The question should be: Does the channel effectively provide information that is useful, inspiring, and life-affirming? Does the channel provide insights and information that trigger your own contact with your higher self to provide your own answers?"

James says communing with one's higher self is excellent, but he wishes more channelers would make an effort to commune with higher spirits in an attempt to bring from them evidence that there is life after death. He says everyone in the world would change for the better if we all knew positively that we would live forever.

CHAPTER THIRTEEN

HERE'S TO HEALTH

"Consciousness controls everything," James says. "All matter, which is composed of energy in a constant state of activity, is directed by mind, the overall regulating principle of the system through which it functions. If you constantly think positive, constructive thoughts, your life will reflect it. And you will also feel well, for your entire anatomy tends to operate normally. Negative thoughts cause the opposite reaction. So keep yourself in top condition by thinking happy thoughts and not causing your cells conflict." James is very firm about this.

"You can often cure illness by the proper positive thinking because when you sincerely believe that you are well, your body is motivated to begin to act that way. Watch yourself over a period of time and see if this is not true. There is nothing more effective for good than the constructive thoughts held strongly in your mind."

I told James, "One thing I have especially learned from your lessons is that we have got to take responsibility for ourselves. The words of that song 'Someone to Watch Over Me' are probably favorites with most people; but not all of us find that 'someone.' If we knew guardian angels were hovering about it would help, but so few of us really believe that. Even with them, we have to take hold of our own lives and handle things. And now you seem to say that we have to control our own physical well-being, too, because bad health isn't allowed."

"Well of course bad health happens." James admitted. "It is one of the biggest challenges one has in a lifetime. Those who have sound genes, a strong body and the good fortune not to come afoul of accidents or a debilitating illness are among the luckiest of all humans. Their character-building obstacles will have to come from different directions. It is intensely to be hoped that the ones who must endure life while using an inadequate physical apparatus will have compensations in other areas. But positive thinking will carry them through with considerably less grief, no matter what happens. It may not cure the condition, but it will make it easier to bear."

"There is a good bit of talk today about techniques of visualization," I mentioned. "Sometimes they work and sometimes they don't."

"That is true. But the effort has nonetheless been of value. An individual makes himself into what he is by the way he endures and learns from his tribulations. A weak-willed, whining do-nothing comes out of a lifetime on earth without much progress. One who faces up to his problems and at least tries to solve them is much farther ahead. It is not that you sit down one day and say, 'Today I will learn the lesson of bearing my pain without carrying on about it.' No, but as you accept trauma with the least possible crying and moaning, you are developing character. You learn each of life's lessons, or fail to learn them, by living up to your potential or by neglecting to live up to your potential. If you become aware of this you will not complain about life's problems and griefs. You will understand that they are learning processes. After death you become more conscious of the goals toward which your thinking and actions are aimed. You know, because of your better comprehension of the system, what particular subjects you must concentrate on to develop and grow more fully. I would like to recommend that you also attempt this same procedure now. If you wish to live so that you have more success on earth and a head start in future planes of existence you have only to decide to operate that way. When you make up your mind that you will expend the effort to keep your life on a constructive path and maintain your thoughts under control, you can learn to do so. While it is hard work, it is not a great deal more difficult than to give up a bad habit or to acquire a new talent or capability.

"The way you think can affect your body as quickly as germs can, making it ill if you have become angry too easily and too often, or if you have hated too much, or if you have despaired or feared too much. Natural laws are in operation here as everywhere else."

In today's world sometimes even medical men can bring themselves to think along these lines. In the *Arizona Daily Star*, Sunday, February 14, 1989, Bill DeLong, a chaplain at the University Medical Center and a member of the hospital's heart transplant team, is quoted as saying: "There's something about a mind's ability to control the body." He can't put his finger on just what it is, however. "We're talking about the integration of spirit, mind and body — how do they all come together to affect the healing response?"

"And what does mind mean?" DeLong asks. "To me, it's society's attempt to stay scientific and yet still acknowledge the spiritual and emotional boundaries."

"But does a spiritually centered life promote health?" he was asked.

DeLong flashed a sheepish grin. "We've already decided we're better at asking questions than answering them," he said.

It isn't likely that DeLong would care to chat with James about this, but wouldn't a conversation between them be interesting?

Shirley MacLaine, the attractive Oscar-winning actress who has awakened modern interest in the psychic and especially in channeling, is the subject of an excellent article in *American Health* (Jan./Feb. '87) which says: "But whatever you think of her, it's undeniable that Shirley MacLaine has hit a national nerve. While dozens of 'channeling' books now talk about occult encounters, MacLaine has reached far beyond this underground of mystics. She's made it semi-chic to talk about experiences that challenge conventional scientific and religious beliefs — but that millions of Americans share."

The article continues: "I couldn't help asking if the acute body awareness MacLaine gained as a dancer acted as a bridge to her spiritual awareness. She's been dancing since age five, runs seriously to get in top shape and does a daily hour of yoga....

"She insists that it's the soul, not the body, that is the bridge to everything. But, she says, 'When you're physically aware, as an athlete or a dancer would be, it's not long before you realize that your physical well-being is directly connected to your consciousness, to spiritual well-being. You feel good in your mood, your attitude, and you feel better in your body. It's real simple.'"

I salute Shirley for maintaining that it is the soul and not the body that is the bridge. And I'm happy that she has the remarkable health she has. When I watch her dance I'm purely and simply envious. I have seldom in all these years since

I was twenty-six and had the strep blood poisoning, been able to push my body to make it do such invigorating things. I've wanted to, but just to keep moving from here to there without falling apart was all I could do. Whenever I got desperate and attempted exercising, I always pulled or twisted or broke something that retarded my progress instead of advancing it.

So here's Shirley saying to use the body to help us spiritually, and here's James going the same route and insisting that thinking correctly can keep the body well. And here's me expecting Brownie points for just hanging in there. Sure anyone can think well when feeling well. However, no matter how much I fuss about the advice, I realize that MacLaine and James are right. I find that the more I think correctly, the better I feel. It really works.

"Your body wants to do what you tell it," James wrote. "Your consciousness is the master of the mechanism through which it operates. It has to be obeyed, and it is obeyed if you are able to keep your thoughts on your goals. But it is a technique that cannot be successful without work and effort. When you firmly believe that your body is well and happy, it is motivated to begin to act that way. Watch yourself over a period of time and see if this is not true. There is nothing more effective than the constructive thoughts you hold strongly in your mind."

I had to argue, though: "I still say it makes a difference what kind of illness you're suffering. When you're down in bed with the flu, you're not going to be thinking about anything but blowing your nose and wondering where the aspirin bottle got to."

"Well, of course," James replied. "It goes without saying that there are certain times and situations that all the positive thinking in the world won't cure. I know it is not easy when you are in discomfort or pain; but you can still endure it better if you stop feeling sorry for yourself."

James declares he really does understand that practicing his teachings is altogether different from dictating them to a typewriter. "But it is good for you people to know all this now, because in the Etheric plane you will definitely have to apply consistent constructive thinking to *everything*." Underline that, he says. "If you can get a head start here and now you will be much farther along in the next plane. When you say to yourself every morning, 'I am a whole, healthy mind in a whole, healthy body' and keep that thought going all day, you will find that it works."

"You can say that again," I put in, knowing quite well that he would. (James maintains that he is repetitious for the purpose of emphasis.) But then I played devil's advocate: "Still, no one wants a guilt trip laid on him because he's tried all this and it hasn't worked. I'm a good example. You'd be surprised that some people think I don't want to get well because I'm not trying hard enough. They look at me walking with a cane and sneer because I'm putting out books that teach positive thinking and healing and then not practicing what I teach. I'm sure no one wants James or Shirley MacLaine or even Dr. Norman Vincent Peale doing that to them."

"Don't be self-conscious," James replied. "Nobody's pressuring anybody except out of love. You know you already find things easier with the application of the Natural Laws I have told you about. You have seen in your own life how changing your attitude and attempting to follow my suggestions has improved your condition. You must share that with everyone. I would like you to mention some of the instances when you began to make these changes in your lifestyle and found them successful."

Well, the inspiration of James' philosophy has carried me through several recent painful episodes; and although it hasn't cured anything, it has helped me hang on. When feeling miserable it really doesn't do much for a gal to have a spirit breathing down her neck with pep talks, because she's probably too uncomfortable to even know he's there. And when she calls the angels she can't see them fly in on wings of love. What works is that instinctive knowing that someone cares and that all is going to come out right because she's been so indoctrinated in positive thinking and faith in God's mercy workers.

James said to tell how this applies in my life, so I'll mention just two instances. I broke my coccyx (tailbone) a couple years ago. Sat on a round chair and it spun me off onto the floor. It hurt some, but the hard part was that I had to use a rubber ring-shaped cushion for several months.

Now, I almost always wear caftans — classy long, loose robes that are cool for the hot Tucson weather and hide a multitude of physical defects. Also I drive a white 1962 Cadillac Coupe de Ville with fins. It is known as my White

Swan. In car years it is almost as old as I am, but I'll cherish it to the end — its or mine. With all that and my canes, one would think I'd be used to being conspicuous, but lugging that rubber ring around everywhere couldn't help but be embarrassing. I had to apply positive thinking in order to make myself believe I liked it. Actually, I sort of flaunted it, called it my whoopie cushion and carried it openly wherever it was necessary — even to the opera one night.

There was another experience that revealed my faith that I was being cared for by someone somewhere, probably a guardian angel type. At 3 A.M. one time in late July, 1987, I awoke with a kidney stone attack. That's pretty painful. It's famous for it. I identified the particular agony in my low back from a previous bout, so telephoned my doctor.

"Get over to the Emergency Room right away," he said. So I drove myself the five miles to the hospital. My helping hands were definitely with me, for the pain let up enough to allow me to control the car with no trouble. The minute my body hit the stretcher, though, it came back with extra force and made up for lost time. Tests revealed a small kidney stone that was removed a few days later. But a friend drove me to the hospital that time.

Around 1977 I decided to write a book about psychic and spiritual healers; and shortly afterward a woman I met mentioned that charismatic healing had changed her life. That term was new to me and I queried her about it. A couple days later an editor I was dickering with phoned to say they would publish my projected book. He asked, "Have you heard of charismatic renewal healing?" I said, "Yes, just barely." He said, "Well, the publisher is Catholic and he wants a chapter on it, if that's all right with you." It was.

The next morning's newspaper announced a Catholic charismatic renewal retreat the following weekend at Picture Rocks, a lovely nearby place for seminars and other gatherings. So that Saturday I was there with notebook and pencil in my purse and a tape recorder slung over my shoulder ready to report on this new phenomenon. And almost immediately I discovered an unusual amount of love surrounding me and quickly realized these people had something good going that I needed to learn about.

Chanting in tongues, voices blending together harmoniously into an inspiring eulogy, particularly delighted me. Without a specific tune, each person sang out sounds and syllables that had no definite meaning but all somehow came together melodiously. The priest explained this to me later as "simply exulting in the Lord, in the tradition of the Gregorian chant."

A healing service concluded the first evening's program, and, being on crutches at the time, I was one of those to receive attention. All twenty-five persons present gathered around, some holding hands in a circle and some with their hands on my head and shoulders as I sat in a chair in the center. As they prayed and chanted in tongues, my eyes fogged up. I felt I simply had to be healed just because they wanted it so much. Unfortunately, my various complaints ignored this gracious attention; but I personally found myself headed in a new direction.

CHAPTER FOURTEEN

ALL GODS ARE ONE GOD

After the retreat I read books that informed me further on charismatics and questioned myself about whether or not it would be a good idea to try to have personal experiences investigating this. I learned later that one is not supposed to come to it through intellect, but through blind faith — something of which I have not an ounce in my entire body. The charisma, of course, are the gifts of love from the Holy Spirit. They consist of the divining of spirits, laying on hands for healing, working of miracles, prophecy, and speaking in tongues. I was familiar with these others through my psychical research, and I loved the chanting in tongues, so was open to receiving that.

But could I accept their main premise — Jesus Christ as Savior? I had never discussed the subject with James and didn't know just what he would say about how Jesus fits into Ultimate Perfection's universe. I would never be able to reject this. I was by now too imbued with it. But couldn't I accept Jesus anyway, without worrying about just where He stood in James' hierarchy? I thought perhaps it might be done.

One night I was in great pain with a misbehaving tendon or something that felt as if a sharp knife were sticking into my upper right arm. It had pestered me all day and nothing I had rubbed on, or taken internally had relieved it; and any positive thoughts about it were long gone. So I was lying in bed reading a book about Jesus and the Baptism in the Holy Spirit and decided to try James' way one more time. I talked to the pain and told it to go away, insisting that every cell in my arm and body was filled with God's light and love; but it kept on hurting.

Finally I laid the book down and said, "Well, all right then, Jesus, will *you* please stop this pain?" It stopped instantly, and hasn't returned.

Needless to say, after that dramatic experience I was ready! I started going to Evangelical churches to see if I could

115

get the Baptism in the Holy Spirit. It is true that many people have hoped for this for years without success. Perhaps it was because I was in such a completely receptive condition that it came to me on my first try. During a Wednesday night service at an Assembly of God church I responded to an altar-call, and while the minister was holding my hands and praying over me in tongues, I blacked out for an instant. This was the moment when I apparently let myself go completely and accepted blindly. Coming to, I spoke in tongues briefly and very hesitantly, apparently too self-conscious to let it pour forth in public; and then I began to cry and to quiver inwardly as well as outwardly. When the minister touched me lightly on the forehead, I fell over backwards into some man's waiting arms. (I had always believed the ministers pushed people, but that is not true.) Even after returning to my seat, and then on the ride home, I vibrated with exhilaration.

The speaking in tongues turned out to be the fun part, when I did it privately at home. It was an "emotional release of a healthy kind" according to Dr. Henry Pitney VanDusen, former president of New York's Union Theological Seminary. I had to practice in order to perform it well, and nothing but nonsense syllables ever came out of me — no unknown foreign languages, I am sure. But it was a reaching out to Divinity without intelligible words and thoughts getting in the way. It was a knowing my oneness with God as I had never quite been able to achieve it before.

So guess what I did. I wrote a book. Don't I always? *The Conversion of a Psychic* (Doubleday 1978) was designed to give the Evangelical Christians the benefit of my thinking about psychical phenomena and charismatics. I had knowledge from personal experience about prophecy, healing, divining of spirits, even miracles of a sort, and now speaking in tongues. All I had been studying in my research of the psychic field over the years was the modern equivalent of what they were learning from the Good Book. And it all indicated life everlasting just as Jesus had confirmed it by His Resurrection. Since I was now one of them, having had the Baptism in the Holy Spirit, they would surely listen to me as I spoke of spirit communication and how it proved everything they believed. They would? Talk about naivete. Talk about self-delusion. If even three fundamentalist Christians read that book I'll be surprised. They were sure the devil made me do it and avoided it religiously.

I found it difficult to believe this reaction, yet it is universal, as Joy Snell points out in *Ministry of Angels*: "...it seems utterly fantastic and almost unbelievable that churches throughout the world — particularly the Christian church, which teaches immortality — should harbor such implacable enmity toward spiritism — which *proves immortality*." She adds that "the entire structure of Christianity is built upon transfiguration, spirit communication, mediumship of an almost transcendental order, and psychic phenomena of every conceivable variety."

In my experience going to Pentecostal churches for a while I discovered their sermons stress more than anything else Jesus's giving His blood for man's sins. It seems to be only at Easter that much is made of His having risen from the grave. My charismatic period was before the exposure of television evangelists, when Jim and Tammy Bakker probably gave the whole movement such a bad name it will never recover. But only recently I witnessed Jimmie Swaggart on TV (before his dramatic fall) stomping up and down the stage (pardon me, the platform) waving his Bible in the air and shouting, "The blood! the blood! the blood!" It must have meant something to his rapt listeners. It didn't to me, because I thought it was dwelling on a negative.

I don't remember how it came about that in late February, 1979, for the first time in over five years I sat down at my typewriter and tried to reach James ... hesitantly I must admit. It was a year after the publication of *Conversion* and I was embarrassed because I thought he might believe that when I "saw the light" I lost my enthusiasm for him and his teachings. To me I had just gained another inspirational dimension to my life, but how would he react? I do recall that I protected myself with a prayer before putting my hands on the keys and asking for him. It was a thrill when he answered and wrote the following:

"This is your guide William James happy to be back with you once again."

"How can I be sure it is you?" I queried.

"You will know it is I because I will continue giving the same type of information I gave in the past. We here understand what you have gone through and are happy for you. To have the Baptism in the Holy Spirit is a moving experience and one to cherish. It is a step forward in your development, a growth experience for which you will always be grateful. It is not possible for me to give you anything about Jesus Christ that will satisfy the Evangelicals, who have determined that He is God. It is true, and yet it is not true. Jesus is one of the highest gods, but there is no man ever born who will not achieve a status similar to His eventually after a long period of growth and development. Here is where the Evangelicals will disagree completely, and since we will be unable to talk to them, let us give them no more of our time. It is the seeking person, who is looking for answers, to whom we are addressing this material.

"I will not try to explain nor classify your experience with the Holy Spirit. It is valuable, but it is not limited to Christians. Those of many religions are able to attain something similar when they come in complete accord with their own potential to reach out to Ultimate Perfection and feel the rewarding return of inflowing power from Above. It comes from God, no matter how one describes his god, but it has nothing to do with dogma or creed. It is a strong identifying with the natural forces of the universe, the god state in whatever terms you understand it. It could come to those of any other discipline who have the desire and receptivity of mind to achieve it. It could be compared in some ways to the 'illumination' which occasionally occurs to occultists and metaphysicians. And then again, an uncivilized native sitting on the beach of his tropical island home may have the same transcendental religious experience as he melds into the starry sky in his imagination and identifies with the natural forces that he understands as God.

"The Christian Bible has been mistranslated so frequently and even its better translations have been misunderstood and misinterpreted. It is correct that Jesus Christ had true glimpses of reality. That is why He had such a head start when He came over here and has advanced to such great heights so quickly. It is in labeling Him the Only God that one errs."

118

"But I love Jesus," I cried. "To me He is truly awesome and wonderful."

"You should love him. He is the great and exalted leader who is Head God of Earth. Call on Him at any time for you are reaching out to Ultimate Perfection when you do and Ultimate Perfection, through Him, will respond. Do not ever feel isolated from Him, for His interests are your world's interests. Those who emulate Jesus are on the right track. When Christians seek to live as He lived and love others as He did, they come over here with a head start. And so I do not in any way denigrate the Christians, only those closed-minded sects who believe they know it all and really know very little.

"Jesus was a blessed man who had learned while on earth truly to love His fellows and was so highly advanced spiritually that when He died He was able to come back to earth to prove to men that they survive death — the greatest single piece of information ever given to mankind. Jesus knew the truth that God is in all people, and this is what He taught. It has all been so mangled and so much emphasis has been put on the wrong things that the whole point of His life has been missed by many.

"Jesus was strongly psychic and able to perform miracles that others could also perform if they were as highly developed. I can only hope that you people on earth will produce more and more good sensitives who are spiritually advanced as well. Unfortunately, many of the mediums who have lived so far have not been spiritually developed along with their psychic abilities. Some day there will be others and they will either be sainted or reviled, just as they have been in the past. Man, as you know, is slow to accept new ideas. We can only keep trying."

CHAPTER FIFTEEN

LIVES OF YORE?

Although in this modern world it is difficult to believe in such concepts as possession by evil spirits, these things do occur, according to James, and more frequently than most people suspect. In such cases, an individual may be so completely taken over by an earthbound entity that his mind is unable to function and the spirit's mind is in control of the body.

Obsession is similar to possession except that it is intermittent instead of continuous. It is more of an overshadowing or influencing the thoughts of the victim than a complete takeover. James says, "A spirit not deliberately intending to cause harm moves in on someone for a specific purpose and uses his body temporarily, as when drunks pass out and then revive with all the characteristics of someone else. It *is* someone else — a spirit craving the taste of liquor — who usurps his body. One who has long dominated a weak person may continue to do so invisibly after death, even to the extent of possessing him. There are occasions when the owner of the body fights back. Sometimes the two consciousnesses may alternate in control of the body. There are some cases diagnosed as hysteria, dissociation, multiple personality, or schizophrenia that are actually attributable to possession or obsession."

This occurs so seldom among normal, busy people that it should cause them no alarm. In danger are those absorbed with vice, crime, addictions, sexual promiscuity, or similar iniquities. "If your demeanor is positive and uplifting," James says, "you will not interest spirits who are looking for trouble. If your life exhibits the finer virtues, there will be no cause to fight for possession of your thoughts ... or bodies."

Unless ... unless you play around unguarded with spirit communication. This idea is well put by Dr. Edwin F. Bowers in *Spiritualism's Challenge*: "Unless you are certain that you are protected by guides who will see to it that no interloper harms you — or obsesses you — you had better not hang out the 'Welcome' sign to every ghostly thug and gangster who may drift into your psychic aura."

Occasionally a spirit might temporarily overshadow someone who is sensitive or psychic and impress his recollections of the past on this person, who then is very likely to suppose he or she is having memories of a former life of his or her own. A good example of this is given in *Your Mysterious Powers of ESP* by Harold Sherman, reporting an instance of a childhood psychic adventure about which Mrs. Dessie L. of Long Beach, California, wrote him. She believes it proves reincarnation, but Sherman has another explanation for it.

When Dessie was a child she was on a camping trip with her father and her brother George. They came to a spot where none of them had been before, where a house had once stood in a leafy vale. Dessie began to battle with herself because she felt impelled to run down the hill. When her father reproved her, she told him, "My dishes are hidden down there" and "My swing was just under the hill." After some argument that she couldn't possibly know what she was talking about, her father and brother went with her to see. She then showed them a tree with the remains of a swing on it; and they dug in the earth where she indicated and found what she described in advance as "Haviland china, white with blue decorations." Her father buried the dishes again, for he was sure the girl's mother would never understand.

"Imagine arriving home with a new set of dishes and telling Mom, 'I found them buried under a tree,'" I remarked.

"A nice set of Haviland china might have made up for any misgivings she had about the strange story," James said.

"Surely they could have taken the chance. It rattles my Scottish bones to think of anything as valuable as Haviland being wasted."

"Men and women often fail to give their spouses credit," James commented wisely.

Anyway, Dessie concluded her letter to Sherman, "I don't know what you will think of this, but to my mind, at least, it is a very sacred story, and positive proof of reincarnation."

Why should Dessie presume it had to be herself in a past life who had hidden those dishes? Because that is the only explanation she knew. Harold Sherman thought he had a better one: "To me, it is ... evidence of possession by a discarnate entity, by one of the persons who lived in the old house that was now rotted away, who had remained there, earthbound, for years with his or her attention, and feelings, fixed on an emotional moment when it was necessary to hide the prized dishes to keep them, possibly, from being stolen by vandals of some sort."

"Reincarnation has more followers than any other doctrine," says James, "having had its origin long ago in the highly populous countries of the Orient. It is rare to find any two persons who interpret it exactly the same way, as there are almost as many reincarnation beliefs as believers. The Yoga concept, more prevalent in the East, is that one has to keep spinning on the Wheel of Life until he sees the illusory nature of earthly desires and achieves complete selflessness. Only then can he escape the cycle of earthly rebirths and achieve nirvana. More often accepted in the West is the more palatable modification that in order to fulfill himself each individual needs to live many times on earth so that he can learn every kind of lesson from having all types of experiences."

"This last theory seems to appeal to lots of my friends," I said.

"Many who are sincerely seeking enlightenment are intrigued by it," James replied.

"Well, yes, they are all wonderful people, but they're just hooked on this idea of having to experience everything in many lifetimes."

"Having other opportunities to accomplish what one was unable to achieve the first time around is very appealing to those who do not know that it is not necessary to make up *on earth* in another life for things not acquired or undergone or learned in this one. It only seems important when it is not recognized that existence in the earliest phases of the Etheric plane is very similar to that on earth. It is during this time of gradual transition that all recompense is made for errors committed, and as one progresses all opportunities longed for are experienced."

"Sometimes just one lifetime here seems forever," I noted. "I can't conceive of wanting to go through it over and over again. In fact, most of those I talk to about it don't want to have to come back; but they seem resigned to it."

"From earth's viewpoint a lifetime is long, but from ours it is not. Actually, in the wider perspective your life on earth is extremely short. In fact, of your entire eternal existence the period that is spent on this revolving ball is roughly equal in comparative length to the first step in a trip around the world at the equator. And you certainly would not wish to retravel that first step over and over again before you went on with the rest of your tour.

"You aim to do the best you can with your time on earth, and so you hope for the type of experiences that will give you the most successful basis for the future. You would not wish to start your trip around the world with no preparation; neither will you want to begin your journey into the afterlife ill prepared. But surely you can see the unimportance of each specific event that happens to you in such a relatively short period of time. It is what you do with each situation in which you find yourself that is of value."

While he has not undergone numerous past lives, this is an "old soul" talking to us in this book. James spent his sixty-three years on earth studying and researching in philosophy, psychology, parapsychology and all related fields while also marrying and having five children. He participated in life to the fullest. Since his passing in 1910 he has continued to learn and to teach for seventy-eight years longer, a total of one hundred forty-one years of quality time, growing mentally and spiritually into a soul of great wisdom and compassion.

James understands the point of view of those who believe they have to reincarnate because they are not satisfied with the person they now are and feel that a number of other lifetimes will make them ultimately more acceptable. He says:

"When I came over here and learned about evolutionary progression I was at first very reluctant to think of myself in the role of one who would live forever, for I felt unworthy to continue as the person I was. And yet now I accept that I will be William James throughout eternity. As I improve and realize that I will continue to improve until I achieve the status of an angel and then eventually a god, a unit of Almighty God Himself, I begin to see that I will have eternal value as the individual I am. The idea grows on you."

GHOST WRITERS IN THE SKY

In 1919 Dr. James H. Hyslop, professor of logic and ethics at Columbia University and one of the founders of the American Society for Psychical Research, wrote "...reincarnation ... does not satisfy the only instinct that makes survival of any kind interesting, namely the instinct to preserve the consciousness of personal identity .... A future life must be the continuity of this consciousness or it is not a life to us at all...."

James said, "It would not be possible for anyone to undergo a number of lives as different people and come out of it clear about his personal identity. It is easy to suggest that he lives the different lives as if he were in progressing grades at school, but this is not the way the system works. When one goes through school, he always retains his awareness of himself as the same individual, even though many of his aspects change as he grows and develops. When one is living a life, he *is* that person, he is not just playing a role or a series of roles; so if he were to go through the lifetimes of a variety of different people, he would end up completely confused about his identity. It is his consciousness that survives, remember, and not just some essence of himself."

After discussing why it is not appropriate for a person to live more than one life, James has to state that, unfortunately, some people do live two lives ... to their utmost bewilderment at the end of their second experience. A spirit who believes he must reincarnate has occasionally moved into the body of a baby just before or just after it is born and, while possessing it, has lived the life that should have belonged to the consciousness destined for that body. When the time comes for this body to die, the spirit who has been inhabiting it is entirely mixed-up. "I have personally seen the evidence of this," James says, "in several confused spirits who have undergone the anguish of trying to straighten out their identities after living two lives. It is terribly confusing for them to understand who and what they really are, for there has been no role playing but the actual reality of being two different people. Those who idealize the idea of living many lives suspect that it will be easy, by some kind of simple process that goes on during the interval between lifetimes, to encompass all the experiences and memories of various existences; but instead it is most difficult."

Particularly in India, where belief in reincarnation is so prevalent, there are cases which would indicate that occasional spirits may attempt rebirth by entering the body of a baby or small child, but possession or obsession is the most likely explanation for this. Shanti Devi, for instance, from Delhi, has been written up frequently as an instance of past-life recall. "It is obvious to me," James says, "that when she was a child she was strongly influenced by a spirit, a young woman named Lugdi who had died in childbirth in the nearby town of Muttra. Believing it possible to come back in another body, and not wanting to leave her newborn son, Lugdi entered or overshadowed a baby born a few years later — Shanti Devi, who began to speak of her past life almost as soon as she was able to talk. By the time she was nine years old, Shanti was so insistent that she be taken to visit her husband in Muttra that her parents complied with her wishes. There she identified Lugdi's husband, her son, and other persons and places in what could only be called a supernormal manner, for Shanti Devi had never before been to the city of Muttra. As the girl grew older the memories of the prior life were spoken of less and less, probably because the spirit of Lugdi had withdrawn her attention."

A very good example of past-life recall is the story of Jasbir, which is correctly reported by Dr. Ian Stevenson in *Twenty Cases Suggestive of Reincarnation* as an instance of possession, although it frequently is mistaken for reincarnation.

Jasbir was a boy who died of smallpox in the spring of 1954 at the age of three and a half. He was to be buried the next morning; but sometime during the night his body stirred and came back to life. Within a few weeks he was well enough to talk, and then it was revealed that his personality and character had changed completely. He ws now speaking in a Brahmin dialect and declared he was someone else altogether, a higher-caste Brahmin.

Jasbir now insisted that he was Sobha Ram of Vehedi, a nearby village. As he grew older he reported many instances in the life of Sobha Ram which were later confirmed, telling how he met his death at the age of twenty-two during a wedding celebration when he had fallen off a chariot and was killed. When he was finally taken to Vehedi, he knew the way to Sobha Ram's home and recognized all the people that young man had known. He was only happy when in Vehedi, so arrangements were made that he could spend most of his summers with the family he claimed to have been his own in his past life.

Dr. Stevenson said he had interviewed all the people concerned in this case and thinks they were telling the truth. It is very clearly an instance of possession in which the deceased man took over the body just vacated by the spirit of the boy. His psychic force was strong enough to enable the body to return to life and usefulness, according to James.

A similar case is erroneously classified as reincarnation by its author Jonathan Cott. *The Search for Omm Sety*, Reincarnation and Eternal Love, is the factual account of the life of a modern woman. When an English child, Dorothy Eady, was three years old, she fell downstairs and was so badly injured she was pronounced dead. Shortly afterward, however, she came back to life with the consciousness and memories of a teenage girl of ancient Egypt, who had been the lover of Pharaoh Sety I. From then on this girl took over the body completely and the child's consciousness was permanently gone. When grown, consumed by her desire to return home, she moved to Cairo and never returned. In Egypt she worshipped the old gods, spent much of her time at the Temple of Sety, and changed her name to Omm Sety. She firmly believed that her Pharaoh lover came to her at night and resumed their 3000-year-old romance.

Over the years, with her intimate knowledge of ancient times and customs, Omm Sety became a respected Egyptologist. Even though she was known as strange, the author says, "the unwavering courage and faithfulness with which she lived her life" made everyone take her seriously and admire her. This, says James, is a clear case of possession, very similar to the Jasbir story where a spirit enters a child's recently deceased body and remains there until death.

A book called *Eternal Progression* by Justin E. Titus says:

"According to Ahura Mazda's ... doctrine of reincarnation, one puts off mortality and corruption by going backward and downward into mortality and corruption, not once, but scores, and hundreds and thousands of times. A spirit would have a difficult time putting off the image of the earthly by repeatedly putting it on again. Such conduct would not help one to assume the image of the heavenly. One assumes the image of the heavenly, not by going backward and downward, but by going forward and upward through the educational grades of the ever-ascending heavens."

CHAPTER SIXTEEN

HOW NOT TO BELIEVE IN REINCARNATION

Nothing had ever been received through mediums about reincarnation until the prevailing philosophy of India was brought to the west just over a century ago. Now channelers everywhere are giving past-life readings all the time because so many people ask for them. Originally the idea of having many lives was thought of as a great disadvantage, but today it is made attractive. It shows wisdom to be an "old soul." It is enchanting to have been all those different interesting people in ages past.

Except for those with firm Judeo-Christian-Islamic traditional religious convictions, many think there is no other theory of an afterlife except rebirth. A woman once said to me at a psychic seminar, "You don't believe in reincarnation? You mean you just believe that when you're dead you're dead?"

Today reincarnation is definitely "in," but I've found many who aren't happy with the idea of having to keep coming back on earth and doing it over and over until they get it right. They are delighted to learn instead of a life of spiritual evolvement in higher planes of existence.

James wrote: "Those who have rejected orthodoxy presume they have no place to go except to the ancient doctrine of many lives in physical bodies on earth. Evolutionary Soul Progression is a third alternative, however, and many who are flirting with reincarnation because they do not know what else to believe will be highly gratified to learn about it. Knowledge of evolutionary progression reveals that undergoing more than one life in order to learn is unnecessary.

"If it is not known that we progress in spirit spheres, then naturally there must be some other intelligent means to continue to live and learn, and the idea of going through numerous lives has strong romantic appeal. It is certainly glamorous to picture yourself as having been a Chinese concubine, a great Persian warrior, or even a slave in the Golden Age of Greece. Because it seems to explain all of life's inequalities, the idea of 'karma' has especial appeal, for karma gives you the opportunity to make retribution for your past sins of omission or commission.

Adherents to the theory of reincarnation believe that your situation in your present life is your personal choice in order to improve conditions that existed in previous lives when you made mistakes or committed crimes and did nothing to correct them. If you were a dissolute Roman emperor, for instance, who caused human beings to die at your whim, you now choose to enter the body of a poor and perhaps deformed baby so that you must suffer intolerable unhappiness. If you blinded men during the Inquisition when you had a position of authority, you may now come back to earth as a sightless child in order to make recompense."

James observes however that "the injustices that are supposedly rectified by causing an evil person to be reborn into a physically damaged body would not necessarily work as karmic recompense, for many who are crippled or blind lead very happy lives full of accomplishment and character growth as they handle their handicaps well. Thus karma can be considered compensation as well as retribution, but James wants the reader to understand that both are accomplished in spirit planes of life, not back on earth in other lifetimes. The inequities of life the reincarnationists complain of are actually opportunities to learn, not punishments."

For a number of years now I have avoided getting into discussions about this subject because I have come to hate arguments. But one man insisted on it, and James wants me to tell our readers about him.

Henry was a neighbor of mine in Florida during one of my sojourns there, and he would come over every morning and sit on my porch and have a mug of coffee with me. Almost every day he'd work the conversation around to the subject of reincarnation, for he was determined to convince me that many lives were necessary in order to enfold a complete person. Nothing could swerve him from this; and he was one of those smug individuals who doesn't hesitate to use the supercilious bromide, "Well, when you are *ready*, you will see that reincarnation is the one and only doctrine." As these discussions continued, he began to insist that the fact that I am crippled is due to karma. Probably in some past life I had undoubtedly kicked someone into a lake and drowned him, or caused some other nefarious crime with my feet.

It so happened that this man had false teeth — the glaringly white, obviously manufactured kind that used to be called "choppers". Finally, goaded beyond restraint one morning, I slapped my coffee cup down on the table, spilling half of it but too agitated to care, and said, "All right, Henry, you've forced me to say this. I'd rather be lame than to have to wear false teeth."

Henry was so startled he got up and started mopping up my coffee with his handkerchief, bustling busily about as he tried to comprehend my point of view. How could I possibly think of my plight in that favorable a light — or his as that disagreeable? And that was just my point. I've learned through my affliction how kind many people are, and perhaps I've acquired more compassion than I might otherwise have had. Mine certainly is an endurable condition. But he thought of it only as karmic retribution. And yet his ugly false teeth to him were no punishment; they were merely a situation he had to put up with — which was my argument exactly.

When I told James this story, he had a great snapper for it. "You missed the occasion for the perfect retort," he said. "You should have told Henry that obviously in a past life he bit someone to death."

Working off bad karma is probably more realistic in spirit spheres than it would be going through another lifetime on earth, according to James, "because a life that has not been lived to the fullest must be reckoned with here by constant effort. One who was only slightly unsuccessful can improve quickly; but a miscreant leads a miserable existence until he begins to learn the reason for the sordid condition he is in and faces up to the work it will entail to make restitution for the crimes he committed. Karma here is expiated by conscious self-improvement, but it is sometimes a long and difficult process, especially for criminals and corrupt persons."

During a pause I was thinking about those unfortunate people in India who have believed for centuries that they must spin around on the Wheel of Life.... Just then James started to type, finishing my sentence for me even though I hadn't spoken a word.

"...never able to stop until they finally learn how to achieve complete selflessness, or perfection, or the nirvana state — however they interpret their goals. They will accept whatever social conditions they find themselves in as their karma. Thus the Untouchables of India never made any effort to throw off their unbearable caste system, believing that such a situation was their own choice in order to work off karma from bad acts in former lives. One or two uprisings would have removed the stigma of this terrible social system long ago. But the lower castes would not try to change their situation because they thought it to be their own responsibility that they were where they were."

James suggests, "Actually, if the idea of karma were true, those who attempt to improve the lot of mankind would have no right to help the poor or the miserable, for it is their obligation to be in the state they are in and they should be allowed to suffer as they have chosen to suffer. So all the good that has been done for others in the world has instead foiled their efforts to pay off their karma by living in a wretched state."

A variation on this theme: I knew a woman once who had a dreadful cat she hated. And the cat hated her and scratched and clawed and bit her at every opportunity. For some reason she was convinced it was her karma to keep the cat and she did, as she daily slathered iodine on numerous long bloody scratches. I've lost touch, but would really love to know what eventually happened. Did she keep the cat until either she or it killed each other? Or, when the wounds became too numerous, did she finally say, "To hell with karma and the cat" and lose it?

If just plain rebirth, without any fancy ribbons or embellishments, is difficult for me to accept, think of that appalling Eternal Return idea of German philosopher Freiderich Nietzsche that everything in the universe keeps repeating itself, down to the minutest detail.

Harold Sherman made a good point in *Psychic* February 1974:

"I used to think that the concept of reincarnation explained the otherwise unexplainable. But as time went on and my experience became expanded, I began to see other possible alternatives. I began to realize we're just beginning to get into the study of genetics and genes and the physical characteristics our ancestors passed on to us. So why, then, if we accept this, can't we accept the possibility that mental and emotional characteristics were also passed on through the genes?"

Sherman points out that purported memories of a past life could then sometimes be "recalled experiences which happened to a direct line ancestor. The mind is a highly imaginative tool and people, under suggestion or hypnosis, can easily dream up what they think they were or would like others to think they were."

Racial memories are inherited not only from parents and grandparents, but also from many generations past. In Titus's *Eternal Progression* the statement is made that "Genetic memories are ancestral memories. Just as you inherit bodily characteristics from your ancestors, so do their life experiences often transmit themselves, through channels of mental inheritance, into your memory. You can very easily mistake the life recordings of your ancestors for memories of your own past lives."

James mentions that genetic memory may produce information about the life of an ancestor when a person is age-regressed by a hypnotist. Yet also, when an individual is hypnotized, a spirit may speak through him just as it would through an entranced medium. The famous Bridey Murphy, who appeared when a woman named Ruth Tighe was hypnotized, was claimed to have been Ruth's memories of a past life. Instead, Bridey was actually an obsessing spirit who moved into Ruth's body and talked while Ruth was hypnotized into a mediumistic trance.

James adds, "I would suggest that you who believe you occasionally have fleeting memories of past lives could actually be overshadowed by spirits, who reflects in your mind memories of their lifetimes on earth."

One evening at a meditation class I attended in New York City, a young woman (I'll call her Hazel) announced reverently, "I was Mary Magdalene!" She explained that she had been hypnotized the night before and age regressed, and this startling truth had been revealed. Hazel had a weak personality, and she couldn't handle a belief in what she considered to be such a great honor. As time went by she began to take on the characteristics and act out the role of the ancient prostitute who loved Jesus, and she soon lost touch with reality. A few weeks later she was a mental patient in Bellevue Hospital.

When a classmate (Jane) heard about this, she asked the rest of us for advice. "I don't know what to do about Hazel," she said. "Years ago when [the great psychic] Edgar Cayce was still alive, I was in Virginia Beach in the waiting room ready for a reading from him when a girl came out of his private office glowing with happiness and announced, 'Cayce just told me I was Mary Magdalene!' Now if Mary Magdalene has already been taken, then Hazel can't have her. I don't know whether or not to tell her. What do you think?"

We thought Hazel should know, and so Jane visited her in the hospital and informed her. This snapped the young woman right out of her delusion, and she was normal after that, as far as I am aware.

"It is quite possible to be a convinced reincarnationist," says James, "until a loved one dies. Then there is additional grief if you do not believe that you will see that dear face again. It is little consolation that he or she might become a relative or friend of yours in some distant future lifetime with no memory of you except, it is presumed, a subconscious one.

"It is wonderful to believe instead that you and your beloved will go on together consciously improving yourselves until you reach the Heights."

James continues: "If you are convinced of rebirth you could very likely waste much of your time that should be spent studying in the school of life because you believe you can do makeups in future existences. You should instead be learning your earthly lessons now, because another chance will never come in a physical body.

"I am not a teacher with a ruler ready to crack your knuckles. Instead I am a very kindly soul with a truth that is different from reincarnation but infinitely more valuable. Listen to me."

CHAPTER SEVENTEEN

BUNDLES OF LOVE

"A child comes into the world with the soul, or consciousness, he has received from God and the body and capabilities he has inherited from his ancestors," James writes. "And the consciousness becomes manifest at birth, not a moment before. The spirit body is the pattern around which the physical body grows in the womb; but there is no conscious awareness within either body until birth. The fetus is a lively little organism that lives, grows and reacts to physical stimuli, but it does not think and does not have a soul until the moment it is born. It is the mother's subconscious mind that controls its functions as long as it is a part of her body. The memories some people believe they have of events that occurred during their time in the womb are retrocognitive psychic impressions only and do not represent the activity of any kind of mental processes before birth."

The night after I received the above paragraph I was lying in bed thinking about it: "Yes, but some people say the consciousness arrives at conception, and some say at the quickening — about twelve weeks after conception. I wonder why it is better to have it arrive at birth."

As this was going through my mind, I had an urge to get up and rush to my typewriter, and the following appeared:

"If you want to give me an argument about this, I have one or two answers. You know, if you stop to think of it, that no mind could endure to be confined in such a small dark space as a womb for nine months. Why, the baby would come out of it with inborn claustrophobia it would never get over."

"But the fetus may be sleeping," I suggested.

James replied, "If a consciousness were in the baby during the fetal period, and if the system had it so arranged that it would spend all of its nine months in utero sleeping, a habit pattern would be so programmed into it that keeping awake would be difficult for the rest of its life."

There was no use my arguing any more, even if I had thought of anything else to say, for James concluded briskly, "No, the arrival of the consciousness at birth is much more logical. And anyway, it is the way things are."

When a baby is born, according to him and to mediums with whom I have discussed the subject, the child's forbears who are interested in it gather around to salute its entrance into the world, just as they also frequently assemble to greet the soul leaving the physical body at death, when it is born into the spirit world. I have heard several psychics tell of being present at the birth of a baby and seeing a glowing light suddenly appear and enter the infant's emerging head.

James says: "The genes the child has from his parents and grandparents and other progenitors determine his physical and mental makeup. He is not discriminated against by an avenging God if he is born without good health or a brain through which his mind can operate successfully. His consciousness is always sound, for it came to him as a 'thought' from God, remember. But if the brain is defective the consciousness cannot function through it normally. And thus we occasionally have those poor little creatures called imbeciles or morons. A reincarnationist would say it is not fair unless they will have another chance to live again on earth in a healthy body. But this is not necessary, for they are handicapped only while on earth. After their death they will have the same opportunities as anybody else. No matter at what age this person passes over, he will be cared for, loved and taught in much the same way as babies are who die. And his progress will be no slower than theirs, for his consciousness is intact. Eventually he will arrive at his Heavenly Destination just as everyone else does."

James went on that people who are not morally and physically fit to bear offspring should be prohibited from doing so. "In a world that has the problem of overpopulation — or in any world, for that matter — sterilization of the unfit is only logical and proper. Also, if a mother contracts German measles or any other disease that will affect the fetus or takes medicine or drugs that will harm it, then she should terminate her pregnancy. It is important that only babies are allowed to be born who have a healthy mind so that they will be mentally able to cope with life. Once you accept the fact that no infant has a sense of awareness or soul until birth, you will be able to consider the idea of abortion without so many qualms, for abortion does not eliminate a conscious human being."

The preceding information about babies was given in 1967 in the first draft of the James material. In recent years the situation of the newborn has become increasingly frightening as the use of drugs and the advent of AIDS have caused the births of so many infants in no condition to cope with living.

In The New York Times, September 25, 1989, Mary Steichen Calderone says, "As a physician, I can see reasons both for and against abortion, but there is one person whose right to abortion has not ever been recognized, much less considered or met: a fetus that has been damaged before birth and will never have a chance for a normal life.

"My concern is for the rights of such innocent fetuses not to be born."

She goes on to say that because of the effect of their mother's consumption of drugs or alcohol, or of being infected by an AIDS-carrying mother, these fetuses were damaged beyond repair, but not beyond life.

"Might such a maimed and distorted human without a future not merit the blessing of quite simply not being born?" Dr. Calderone asks.

I brought such statements as this to my communicant's attention. "The controversy over abortion is very big right now," I mentioned.

James replied: "Try to realize that the baby is only a small figure without a consciousness growing within the mother. Thus it has no individuality or personality and is only alive in a physical and not a spiritual sense. It is much better in case of severe problems to let the little one die than to give birth to an incomplete being. A mother who has a miscarriage can console herself by this same understanding of the situation."

"You make everything sound so simple," I told my friend. "You have a way of getting right to the basics and telling it like it is, even though what you say may not be palatable to lots of people."

"It is just sheer common sense from the point of view of one who sees the overall picture of life in its entirety."

It should be obvious by now that James will come right out with anything he knows to be true, even if it is against church teachings or public opinion. No pussyfooting for him, this spirit has the goal of being completely factual, so we have to realize that he isn't being unkind about babies and their mothers, he is being realistic. He wants us to face up to our responsibilities to mankind and handle them intelligently....

"Let me speak for myself," he interrupted me. "I am by no means an enthusiast for abortion. I only insist that terminating a pregnancy is preferable in some cases to unfortunate alternatives. Certainly all people, especially those who are unfit or unable or underage to become parents, should protect themselves whenever they have intercourse. Using contraceptives is preferable in every way to abortion. But no infant should come into the world who does not have the ability to become a mentally self-sustaining individual. It is difficult for parents to make the decision to abort a prospective offspring who is sure to be severely defective, but it is much more difficult for them to raise a mentally-deficient child. Many parents have spent their lives in misery just because they have given birth to an imperfect infant."

James now went back to the typewriter: "It will not be difficult for a mental defective when he gets to the Etheric, for he will no longer be blemished there. There is no real problem of an eternal nature that is engendered by a child's being impaired or by his dying young. For those who have lost a baby through illness or accident, be relieved by the knowledge that the life of a child raised in the spirit world is much happier than if he had grown up on earth. He has more to learn, in some ways, because he is not subject to the buffetings he would normally have to undergo, which help so much to build character. Still, he can experience vicariously the problems of his family, for he is raised with it — yes, you did not know that, did you? Even while he is in the nursery the tot is cared for by loving spirits right in your vicinity, frequently in the family group, if you only knew it. The spirit playmates of earth children may often be their own brothers and sisters who have passed over.

"Each child who dies is raised in the spirit world with love and understanding," James went on. "He does not have to undergo the heartaches and hardships of life, the emotional frustrations that beset us all, and the problems of trying to understand what life is all about. He gains his personal sense of values, his honor, integrity, and moral responsibility by observation, as it were, rather than by actual experience.

"The parents of a child who has died should never try to put it out of their thoughts in order to keep from suffering over it. Since it will be raised right with them, they should talk to it occasionally and let it know they still love and remember it."

Raising a child properly in today's complicated world is an extremely difficult undertaking, and James understands this as he says, "It will demand all the self-discipline parents can acquire in order to give their offspring a proper foundation so that he can adjust properly to existence."

I agreed with him heartily, but couldn't help but tease him. "You and your reactionary terms," I said. "Self Discipline, Cause and Effect, Evil Spirits, Free Will. The behaviorists will be after your head."

"I can't help it. Those terms are all valid. Just because concepts are old is no reason to reject them. But then again, just because a belief has been prevalent for a long time is no reason to accept it, either. Man has had many glimpses of the truth in the past and he will have many more before he ever gets the whole picture. But eventually every child will be raised knowing how to think properly to bring out his finest capabilities."

"That'll be the day," I said skeptically, musing about Human Nature, another of the old saws he was apparently overlooking.

"Yes, I am an idealist," he wrote. "We all are here where I am. But we have the advantage of knowing about the overall long-range plan of the universe. It is good, believe me, it is good. Whether or not your globe will live up to standard will be in the hands of these very children we are talking about here.

"If all life on earth were peaceful and serene, there would be less for you to do to raise your offspring properly, but it would also be less of a challenge for you. And challenges are what you thrive on. So when you decide for a baby, face the fact that it won't be easy, guide yourself accordingly, and plan to make his earliest days as secure as possible. This is done by loving him so thoroughly and devoting yourself to him so completely that his first years give him nothing but peace and inner serenity. No matter what poor environment a baby is born into, if both his mother and his father (hopefully presuming that he has both) love him and teach him to love others and to think constructively, he will not have all the character problems of his playmates. He will live relatively free of those insecurities that plague others."

I said, "I don't see how even this dream child can have a life without irritations, exasperations, humiliations ... these things that happen to us all no matter how well cared for we are."

"He will have all those, and even genuine misery at times. How else can a person learn? To anticipate growing up without seasoning is ridiculous; but if he has a good start, he can overcome everything. Each individual has to progress as best he can with the abilities he has in the situations in which he finds himself. This does not mean that those who are handicapped or poor are deliberately discriminated against by God. Neither does it mean that they are making karmic retribution for crimes committed in previous lives. It is his use of the capacities with which he was born that makes a man of character; it does not matter what specific problems he has to overcome as he develops.

"There is no reason to bemoan the fate of the poor individual without sight, for instance. Granted that it makes his life on earth more difficult; it is how he accepts it that is important. And do not forget, after his passing, his years in the dark are quickly forgotten as his eyes are joyously opened for the rest of his eternal existence. Each individual has many challenges to meet during his life. If he meets them well when blind — and there are many happy and fulfilled sightless people in the world — he will progress faster than someone who may have started his life with a perfect body yet has done very little with his capabilities. Enduring with fortitude builds character. Others who have no such handicaps may make less of their opportunities."

James concluded: "We have spoken here of defective children so that those who have had to face such sorrows will know that this is only a temporary condition. The joy of a healthy, happy infant cannot be equaled; but in the spirit world after their passing, all children are healthy and happy and headed toward a great and glorious life."

CHAPTER EIGHTEEN

CHILDREN ARE FOR CHERISHING

James says that for parents to raise a child wisely, with love and intelligence, and to make a well-adjusted adult of him, is one of the greatest contributions to the human race. Disciplined parents who set good examples and raise happy children in harmonious surroundings, are themselves happy. And he adds: "If a husband and wife cannot be contented with each other, they should be intelligent enough not to have children. When contemplating a family, the couple should think of the amount of time and effort that will be spent raising it properly. They should not plan for one until they are sure that they are mentally and emotionally mature. If this sounds as though I am trying to reduce the vast masses of the world, why not? Overpopulation is a critical problem, and babies must not be brought into a situation where they cannot be cared for adequately. No couple need feel guilty if they choose not to have any. Instead they should be proud of making a sensible choice."

Right while we were working on a revision of this chapter *People* Magazine (May 9, 1988) interviewed British author Penelope Leach, the "child-care guru". She pointed out the difficulties of raising a child from the mother's point of view. "What's a mother to do?" she inquires. "She is supposed to be nurturer, comforter, disciplinarian, tutor, counselor and friend to her children. Yet she has received no formal training for the job...." Leach says that the task of raising children is the hardest thing a person does, particularly because "small children aren't specialized creatures and it is difficult for adults to live with them."

James' comment about this is, "But let us make it clear that no matter whether she likes her child or not, she must take proper care of him. She can't mistreat him. That is why I say do not have them in the first place unless you truly want them and are willing to put up with them."

"Everybody's so grim," I complained. "Nobody mentions the fun of raising children. We had so many good times at home. Mother and Daddy and I kidded constantly, and we read aloud together, and often played card games evenings. Raising children can be pleasurable, at least part of the time."

"It certainly can," James replied. But then he went on handing it out to us: "Throughout this book you will notice that I am talking as if you are responsible individuals with free will to accomplish what you wish with your abilities. This is because you are just that. All the alibiing in the world about your childhood traumas, et cetera, will not relieve you of one iota of accountability for what you ultimately become. When you face up to this and realize the difficulties you are having because of the way you were raised and because of all the negative patterns programmed into you, can you not see why I demand proper consideration for your children so that their lives will be proportionately easier than yours have been?"

James insists he is not old fashioned, but just traditional in demanding that people should continue to observe the proprieties. Children must be stopped from having children in vast quantities. "Youngsters who have undesired babies are not just pathetic, they are criminals. Today there are prescriptions and condoms that make it possible not to have unwanted children. In a culture where young people are frequently thrown together alone in intimate circumstances before they have learned to control their passions, facing facts and being prepared for eventualities is an indication of intelligent forethought, not unrestraint. Above all, substance abusers *must* stop bringing addicted babies into the world.

Although James is firm about couples not having children unless they can provide the important specifics for them, there is a simple answer for those who ardently desire to expend love on a child. It is adoption.

James continues: "The ideal conditions in which to raise a child are quite demanding. From the time the small one arrives until he is at least seven or eight years old, the parents should consider their own lives secondary. If this sounds impossible to you, stop and think what you are undertaking. You are giving personal identity to and raising an individual who will live forever. He will have a great deal to offer the world if he learns to adjust adequately to life and you provide him with a firm foundation of character. You can help him attain this by supplying agreeable surroundings, pleasant associates, constructive thoughts, and much, much love to enfold him always.

"My last suggestion to parents," James says, "is to begin telling your child about his spirit helpers at an early age and train him in positive thinking. Teach him as soon as he learns to speak to start each day with an aphorism of health and happiness and his life will be more successful in every way. On awakening each morning he should recite, 'Today I will be healthy and happy all day long.' He must learn to say it, not by rote, but as an affirmation as important as his prayers at night. If he begins this very early, even before he can talk plainly, it will be such a part of his life's pattern that he will not think of it as a chore but as a normal routine. His existence will be immeasurably improved because of it.

"Let him know not only that there is a God in heaven but that there are angels who love him and want to help him, even though he cannot see them. Suggest to him that he probably has a guardian angel of his very own. If this rapport with his invisible friends is established in his youth, many of his biggest problems in life will be solved by their able assistance, and it will be possible for him to avoid some of the mishaps that could occur to him without the benefit of their far-seeing viewpoint."

James wants people to encourage any sign that their child is naturally psychic. Let him describe his invisible playmates if he has them. "It would be thoughtful not to sit on a chair if he says the unseen little Tommy is sitting there. In other words respect his differences from the norm in this regard. Psychic ability is a truly great potentiality and should be encouraged just as much as any other talents would be."

If a child has an inherited gifts for music, art, mathematics, or the psychic, spirits with similar interests may take him in charge and become guardian angels to him.

If he is highly talented, then especially gifted invisible assistants will be with him. There is a published account revealing just how this has worked in the life of a modern American violinist, Florizel von Reuter. He was a performer and composer, conductor and music teacher who was a violin prodigy in his youth. His mother was confident his musical talent occurred because before his birth she passionately wanted it for him. The name best known to her was Nicolo Paganini (1782-1840), and so she implored his spirit to guide her unborn baby, beseeching him night and day for his influence. When the child was born, she dedicated him to the ideal for which she had prayed. Florizel accepted the responsibility from his earliest youth, amazing his teachers not only with his skill but also with his feats of memory. He often spoke of someone who was with him when he practiced. "Some old master is always listening," he would comment. "I mustn't disappoint him."

Von Reuter said in his book *Psychic Experiences of a Musician* that it was not until he was thirty that he began his search for survival evidence. One of his first spirit communicators was Paganini, who spoke at a voice sitting (where spirits are able to speak aloud through the medium). Florizel was told, "There is a great violinist present who wants to greet the young man. He says his name is Paganini." Then the spirit of the old violinist, speaking through the medium, thanked Florizel's mother for having influenced him to become interested in the child and his music.

Mrs. Von Reuter, also present at the séance, said, "Florizel plays all your twenty-four caprices."

"I know," was the answer. "I have often been present in concerts where he has performed them."

Florizel von Reuter says he doesn't doubt it for a moment. Sometimes when he was playing the violin he had felt his hands moved to a better fingering than the one he had in mind, and he knew it was Paganini helping him.

"If you have an offspring who is psychic," James writes, "see that he is schooled in the areas in which his special abilities lie, for he is often creative and a means of expression is vitally necessary to his well being. Above all, never let him feel that you consider him odd. Foster the growth of healthy roots and you will see fine results in later years. Be sure, however, that your child is warned not to talk to his playmates about his guardian angels. They should be as personal and as little discussed as his other private habits."

I said, "James, you know that a child raised with only love and compassion and guardian angels will be absolutely clobbered when he gets with those little monsters in school."

"I hope he will not be," he replied. "By the time he is of school age he should be warned that his new associates have not been taught all the wonderful things he knows and that he must not worry if they do not understand. He should feel sorry for them instead. Then, with his inbred warmth and loving personality and serenity of spirit he will probably win over even the most arrogant, although he will be self-sufficient enough to be happy without their approval if he should not gain it. Do not anticipate any additional troubles for this little individual who has been indoctrinated correctly since infancy. His life will be an example for all to follow. He will have his share of unhappiness, unforseen developments of one kind or another, deaths in his family and the like, but his backlog of personal security and harmony will carry him through anything."

Prospective parents are told: "If you and your spouse do not care to live your private lives with wisdom, that is your business, but if you take on the responsibility of giving birth, then it becomes someone else's business. This someone — your child — should be the most important person in the world to you. He demands and must have the very best that is in you at all times. If you do not provide him with affection and wise attention, you are neglecting your duty, no matter how well you feed, house, and clothe him and how much money you spend on him. Money, I need not tell you, makes life more comfortable and easier to bear, but it does not provide character. That is acquired only through strenuous effort.

"The wonderful thing about it is that when you exert yourself wisely for love of someone else, your own character develops without your even being aware of it."

CHAPTER NINETEEN

QUESTIONS AND ANSWERS

Here are some questions that friends who have read these manuscripts have asked James to answer:

QUESTION: "What happens to animals? Do they continue to live after death?"

ANSWER: "The animating spirit of life comes directly from Ultimate Perfection into each living thing, which always continues to exist in its spirit counterpart after the death or disintegration of the matter in which it was encased on earth. For this reason the Astral plane looks exactly like your natural world, for it has a duplicate of all the living things of earth. Only the consciousnesses of human beings progress to become components of the Divine, however.

"Those of you who love particular pets will be glad to know that they can remain with you. When you pass into the spirit world your cats, dogs, horses, monkeys, birds, or any other pets upon which you have lavished affection, accompany you when they die if that is what you wish. It is your love of them that enables them to continue to remain with you. If you desire it, they may even stay with you as you progress to higher planes ... and some dogs and cats, particularly, have gone with their spirit friends to very high advancement."

(My mother has told me that my little Junior has remained right with me ever since he died, and I am eagerly looking forward to seeing him again. Soon, I hope.)

James' answer goes on: "When an animal is killed or dies, it does not know it, for its awareness continues to exist in its spirit body."

"Consciousnesses never arrive in a human being after progressing upward from the lower animals. There is no such thing as transmigration of souls either up or down the intellectual scale. No human infant has ever received a consciousness that had formerly lived as any other aspect of life, and no man is ever sent back to live as an animal."

QUESTION: During the time that President and Mrs. Reagan were being harassed about their belief in astrology, I asked James, "Is there really anything to astrology?"

ANSWER: "There is more to astrology than meets the eye, because it deals with aspects of existence that are largely unknown. I am not going to claim that it is scientifically oriented to the point that science will soon accept it as a brother discipline. However, astrological charts are frequently more accurate than chance would suggest. It is often possible by using the procedures employed to learn a great deal about an individual and his future; but someone who knows the techniques would have to explain it to you, I cannot. Accept it that astrology is of value and will be better received as time goes on and more is learned about the universe. The daily horoscopes in the newspapers, however, do not represent astrology either correctly or fairly."

QUESTION: "It is difficult to believe that some persons who have been responsible for genocide and mass persecutions can ever achieve Ultimate Perfection. Are you sure there is not some kind of eternal punishment for these?"

ANSWER: "There is definitely a hell for such human beasts, and they endure in it for a long, long time before they finally begin to make amends, as much as it is possible to make amends, for the terrible tragedies they have caused. Their hell is not one of fire and brimstone, but of hatred and bitterness and misery among others as loathsome as they. Existence seems entirely without hope for them until they begin to realize the depths of their degradation; but eventually they will face up to the extent of their crimes. And someday they will start on the upward path, for nothing negative can ever be eternal. So great is the love of Ultimate Perfection for humanity that all are included, no matter how low they might once have been. Even regenerated mass murderers will one day receive the forgiveness of other advanced spirits and begin trying to learn to forgive themselves, and then they will start their progression. Remember, I told you that God does not

146

want to lose any part of Himself, so each must return to Him eventually as a perfected spirit.

"It is also true that some of such criminals are actually insane. Their minds have been unable to function properly during the times they were in positions of power and they were not capable of thinking intelligently about what they were doing or ordering others to do. Those who because of their greed and avarice have allowed insane persons to hold positions of power are also at fault and will have even more remorse when they realize what they have done. The insane are cared for here in hospitals or nursing homes until they finally return to normal. Some take longer than others; but all will eventually regain their proper manner of thinking and begin to advance.

"Imagine the great love of humanity demanded of the workers who staff these hospitals, when they realize that they are having to assist in the regeneration of a Hitler or a Nero and must always provide them with compassionate care."

QUESTION: "If God is All-Encompassing Perfection, how can He allow such imperfection to exist?"

ANSWER: "There is an explanation for this: If all were perfect, there would be no way for improvement, and God — Ultimate Perfection — is always improving and expanding. Negatives exist so that positives can be recognized. It would not be possible thoroughly to understand Good if we did not have Evil as a contrast.

"When Ultimate Perfection decided to personify certain aspects of Himself, He chose to use the form of Man for this purpose. As man lives he has emotions of all kinds so that he can comprehend all varieties of experience, although he does not have to undergo them all personally. He must come to understand goodness and love; but he must also know the contrast of evil and unwholesomeness, for how can he truly know perfection unless he is aware of imperfection? If one were born perfect and had no life on earth where evil exists, would he be able fully to appreciate the Heights when he attains them?"

Or as Pope John XXIII said, "If God created shadows it was in order to better emphasize the light."

QUESTION: "But why is there so much evil in the world. Why so many evil people?"

ANSWER: "As each baby is born it is supplied with a new thought from God, which is its consciousness or soul. But the body is inherited from its parents and has all the accumulated characteristics of its ancestors within it. The character of an individual is the result of his inherited traits and his upbringing. In the bodies of the numerous descendants of the original two persons who started a family strain, there are so many different combinations of genes that wide variations in character and personality occur. There is no way to regulate the traits that will accrue in the genes of each individual. And each individual has free will and human emotions, which lead to all kinds of actions — good and bad. Evil comes about because man is given free will and allowed to run his life as he pleases. Greed is one of the biggest causes of all crimes — that and sex to excess. Cause and effect is in operation here as everywhere and the results are not always good. But there is only one way to change the situation — always provide good causes in order to have good effects. That is why those who are unfit to bear offspring should not be allowed to do so, and good parenting is a requisite."

QUESTION: A friend who has read your scripts asks why an individual with a good bit of spiritual development might not decide to take his own life in order to hurry into a future existence where things will be easier because he won't have a body to care for or the worries of making a living. With the advancement he has now, wouldn't this individual be able to start his progression right away? So even if suicide caused harder work for a while, would it not be worth it?

ANSWER: "While understanding that I have made the higher reaches of the Astral so appealing that one might have a desire to hurry to the afterlife, I can only think of this question as indicating an extremely juvenile point of view. Of course suicide is totally ill advised. Killing yourself is as bad as killing another, and that is absolutely wrong. Whatever you have not learned because of the deliberately shortened life experience must be made up in the Etheric plane in ways so much more difficult that, believe me, it is better to stick it out where you are, even if conditions there seem to you to be unbearable.

"You must realize that nobody escapes any of his problems by committing suicide; he quadruples them instead. A man has a responsibility to everyone he loves and even to those he just barely knows if his life somehow might affect them. It is his obligation to himself as well as to them to fulfill every commitment as completely and successfully as possible. If he does not do this on earth, he must conclude it in the spirit world. And the extra problems he places on others by his suicide are his responsibility, too. He has to find ways to make amends for them, even though it might take him hundreds of years."

In his recently published book, *The Rising Tide of Suicide: A Guide to Prevention, Intervention and Postvention*, Dr. Louis Richard Batzler writes: "Many suicide victims in their communications from the other side advised against suicide, regretted their act and indicated that, given the opportunity, would never repeat it." He also states: "Most information indicates states of turmoil, fear, struggle, confusion, regret, pain, darkness and an intensification of the psychical torments that drove the victim to suicide. The suicide is described as an interruption and set-back ... a rejection of the souls' will and its plan for a life pattern. It is a premature foreclosure on life. Those who commit suicide destroy the physical vehicle, but do not fulfill the years of their destiny."

James goes on: "Make no mistake, nothing good can ever come of suicide, and a terrible amount of unhappiness, misery, and misfortune is always caused by it. No matter how miserable he may become, no one in his right senses should ever allow himself to take this way out of his difficulties. And certainly do not ever consider it because you think you have achieved enough advancement on earth and are ready for the joys of future existence. That would be the most fantastic misconception of all. Enduring the situation you are in to the best of your ability makes for much faster and easier progression later. Suicide is such an appalling act that I can not say enough against it. DO NOT EVER THINK OF IT."

QUESTION: "It seems as if men are becoming more brutal towards women and children today. Isn't there more wife beating, child abuse and rape than in the past?"

ANSWER: "Because of the breakdown of family life and the fact that so many children run away from home today, there is probably more. But throughout history there have been terrible crimes against women and children that have not been recorded. Now public awareness, bringing it out into the open, means that there will be more activity against it; although many who have this problem even today will not speak of it. It is not likely that such terrible crimes will ever be stamped out entirely until the millennium; but it can be one of your primary goals for world improvement."

QUESTION: "Did Atlantis really exist?"

ANSWER: "What you call Atlantis once existed, but so did a lot of other continents. Many changes of the earth's formation have occurred since the beginnings of time on your planet, and Atlantis is only one of the many civilizations that have been here. Much has been made of it, but it is of no more importance than the others. There were continents in the Pacific with civilizations of a high order, long before Atlantis. The continental drift is an earlier movement of land masses. After the continents separated, Atlantis and several other small continents appeared in the Atlantic. They were destroyed by cataclysms. Conditions inside the earth are in a constant state of motion and there will again be many erupting volcanos and other devastations. It is not up to you current denizens to completely disrupt everything with your nuclear fission, however. By all means speak out whenever you can against it."

QUESTION: "What is the truth about Akashic Records (or the concept that there are eternal records of everything that has happened on earth)? Do they exist?"

ANSWER: "Akashic Records are a concept that has an element of truth. There is no big record book in the sky, but memories and imprints of events continue to survive. All men and women who have ever lived on earth or other inhabited planets still exist in Ultimate Perfection or in spirit planes of existence. And their memories are intact. So everything that has occurred to any of them in their lifetimes is still in their memories; and these could be called Akashic Records.

"There is also the fact that the energy from everything that has occurred still remains in the original form. I have spoken of the beauties of nature here and the animals as well as humans who still continue to exist. This is because nothing in nature is ever eliminated. Earthly happenings of strong emotional force, like a murder or a rape, endure separate from memories of the persons involved, for the force of the event has caused it actually to be formed in time and space. This explains occasional sightings in haunted houses. When anything continuing to exist is sensed by a psychic, he or she is frequently said to be reading the Akashic Records."

CHAPTER TWENTY

IS GOD ANGRY WITH US?

Today people are heard to wonder if God is mad at the world. I asked James and he wrote in reply: "Knowing what you now do about the great force of love and peace that is Ultimate Perfection, you must be aware that He could never be angry. The angels and gods who are involved with earth are certainly chagrined at the condition the world's inhabitants have gotten themselves and their planet into, but they are not mad. They are always trying to help, not judge. And yet you are in the midst of such a period of crisis that it is no wonder many are sure God is disappointed in you."

I wanted to see what he was going to suggest to improve the condition. "How can we fix it?" I asked. "It seems to me we would be better off if we just started over."

James didn't give me any argument about that. "Besides your atmosphere being polluted, many of your people are also polluted — by sexual immorality, pornography, obscenity, those who do not care what terrible diseases they are spreading if their own selfish needs are satisfied." He was obviously not going to stop enumerating our problems: "And we cannot forget terrorism, street gangs gone wild, apartheid, businessmen who are so eager for financial gain that corruption is rampant. I am particularly incensed at the widespread lack of moral fiber."

"Everybody I know says the same thing," I told him.

"What are they doing about it?" he shot right back at me verbally; then he went on typing with hardly a pause: "Your dreadful drug situation is one of our biggest concerns for you because it is out of hand. So an all-out war on drugs should be one of the world's highest priorities."

It wasn't that I didn't agree with him, but I had to report that there seems to be an increase today in the popular incentive for fighting drugs. So I said, "I read about it in every newspaper and magazine and see it on television constantly."

152

"I know, but it is imperative that public opinion be further aroused," James went on, "so that more citizens will offer assistance and more funding will be provided for mandatory treatment and education. Severe measures must be used by national as well as local governments of all countries to stop the drug traffic, and suppliers will have to be the object of stringent law enforcement."

He paused as if for breath (Memo: ask James sometime if spirits breathe), then went on with his chastising: "Addicts must be helped before they are responsible for a much wider spread of AIDS and for further increasing the desperate crime situation. If necessary, junkies should be rounded up off the streets or wherever they congregate and put on special rehabilitation programs or held in custody. I know this will not be popular with civil rights activists, but those who won't take care of themselves have to be taken care of by the rest of you."

I could picture me in my long flowing caftan marching up to some scrawny-looking dope-head, waving my cane at him and saying, "Come with me, young man. I'm going to rehabilitate you."

"I am well aware of the difficulties," James wrote. "Nonetheless my main premise is *individual* [underline that, he says] responsibility. It is so important for the many to become involved in helping the others who need it desperately. What is required is more alarmed citizens."

I recalled something that had happened last summer that would show James just how much good one individual could do for this cause. I'd let him know what really happened when one person (namely me) tried to get rid of a couple of drug pushers who moved in across the hall. Last June my investigative reporter's eye viewed another side of life when new neighbors took the apartment opposite mine. They were two nice-looking young men. One I later learned was just out of high school, the other about twenty. They were well dressed, fresh faced ... the kind of kids you'd like your daughter to bring home to meet the family.

That impression didn't last long. Soon it sounded as though they were going in and out of their house constantly until I realized it wasn't just them but dozens, twenties, thirties, then hundreds (I counted) of other people. And they all banged the door. A door that slams loudly in the wall adjoining yours can lift you right out of your chair. And this is not pleasurable when it happens with frequency. After a week of it, I knocked at their apartment and asked politely if they'd please try to keep their guests from banging and slamming. I was graciously invited in and offered a drink, which was only straight Pepsi so forget it. My neighbors were very pleasant, but their home reeked of marijuana.

Well, the crowds continued. All day and all night cars drove up and waited with their motors running while someone ran in to make a quick purchase ... and bang the door. Vast quantities of young people of assorted sizes, shapes and colors were in and out all day and up until 5 o'clock in the mornings. Oddly enough, they were all average appearing. I mean that there were none who looked like shady characters, nor stereotypes of drug addicts or even casual users. So much for type casting.

Their nightly parties were binges. Girlish shrieks of potted delight or cracked confusion filled the air, the apartment, the entryway, and the parking area outside. Once I heard someone mention "crack", so there was heavy stuff going on, especially noticeable when girls started shouting and crying and being sick. The men were noisy, too; but female voices, when under the influence of one thing or another, can have a shrillness that penetrates the eardrums, especially if one is trying to sleep nearby. Twice men knocked on my door by mistake at 1 or 2 A.M. I didn't care for that either.

Several times other neighbors and I called the security guard to break up noisy parties, but that's all the attention these two ever received from officialdom. Because, yes, sure I had phoned the police. I was told dope peddling wasn't their province, so I contacted 88 CRIME. One officer there allowed me to talk to him several times, but evidently never felt the dilemma worthy of investigation.

Finally the management of the apartments got so many calls of complaint that they, too, became upset. They said, "Mercy, mercy, we can't have such goings on in our high-class complex." So they started trying to evict the tenants. It is hard to believe but they couldn't legally put them out just because of excess noise or suspected drug sales. Luckily the youths didn't pay their rent on time, so the manager obtained a court order and evicted them for that. And I started sleeping again nights.

"There now, you see," I complained when I finished relating my story to James. "I phoned the police, called the security guard, talked to others, went to the office — all more than once. And this alarmed citizen got exactly nowhere."

"You got rid of them, didn't you?" he asked. And, by golly, I had.

"Along with drugs comes the scourge AIDS," James went on. "Those who think this disease was deliberately invented to punish mankind are wrong. AIDS is a terrible affliction, but it was not sent from God to discipline those badly in need of discipline. People will have to do that for themselves. Nature produces events that keep the population from over-expanding completely, but they are normal effects of causes of a natural kind such as hurricanes, earthquakes, volcanic eruptions, or droughts. In the case of AIDS a virus appeared, possibly in a breed of monkeys in Africa, and it was transferred to humans long ago by a bite. It has now been spread worldwide by high-risk sexual practices and drug users. Unfortunately others with normal lifestyles are also being contaminated. It is a situation that won't be cleared up until most people begin to use self-control and discipline. As I have been trying to indicate throughout this text, those are among the desired requisites for successful living anyway. It is essential that all of you who read this pay attention. Help to see that laws are passed to control the spread of AIDS even if it means locking up all drug addicts. These would seem like drastic measures, but it is a drastic situation. Each of you should be making every effort to influence your public officials to stop nuclear fission, to eradicate the drug trade and AIDS, to reduce fossil fuel emissions, to get rid of acid rain and protect the atmosphere's ozone layer and the rain forests."

To reinforce this I told James I had read a quote from Norman Cousins I thought he'd enjoy. "All things are possible, once enough human beings realize that the whole of the human future is at stake."

James really liked that one. He said, "That's exactly what I've been claiming. Hooray for Norman Cousins!" Then he added: "I am very much aware that there are those who think the expectations for mankind in this book are naive. They are thoroughly convinced that the customs that have continued throughout history will never change. I realize the tremendous challenge it will be for you and future generations to make improvements, but I have hopes that it can eventually be done. I am not able to predict the future. As I've said before, we over here can only see trends. But unfortunately the present trends are very disheartening. Yet as a dedicated positive thinker I have to deny the appalling evidence I see before me. If you people become alarmed and aroused enough at conditions and determined enough to improve them, you can do it. It is true that each advancement will have to start with one man here and one woman there; but eventually enough will work together to save the world. It won't be easy and it will take a long, long time, but it can be done. As for now, each individual must try to alert others to the dangers and then do whatever he can personally to take action.

"And call the angels!"

CHAPTER TWENTY-ONE

THE END IS JUST THE BEGINNING

Whenever James gives us a bitter pill, he puts a little sugar on it. "While many conditions today are particularly alarming, during the present century much that is encouraging has occurred. Even now as each year passes it can be seen that many of you are attempting to improve the lot of others. Social advancement is now more rapid than at any time in the history of the world — in civil rights movements... "

I interrupted: "People are on fire all over the world for their civil rights. Many of the Third World countries are aflame."

"Terrible as fighting is," he answered, "it seems somehow to have always been a necessity in the name of human progress. Benign rulers who lead their countries to modern civilization are rare. But, here, look at your women's efforts to emancipate themselves. They are becoming successful by peaceful means. Females have been looked on as second-class citizens all through history. Today they are asserting their rights and making claims of equality with men, which they certainly have deserved all along and never attempted to achieve before.

"Less than one hundred twenty-five years ago slavery was accepted as proper by the majority; today the status of blacks has improved tremendously, although it still has a long way to go. Consider the plight of the insane who, until the last century, were treated as criminals and chained in prisons While conditions in institutions, and on the streets, are still bad, the change in the general attitude toward them is noticeable. Each year citizens are becoming more cognizant of the needs of the poor, the helpless, the handicapped. This is so obvious to me in comparison to the way things were when I lived on earth. In my lifetime child labor was still prevalent. Today look at ecological awareness — you at least talk about the problems now — and your concerned young people. The Peace Corps is an excellent step forward."

James even tries to pacify us a bit about the sexual situation he so sadly deplores. "History shows us that strong movements in one direction are usually counterbalanced by equally strong movements in the opposite direction. Morality sways back and forth; but in civilized cultures it has seldom gone as far toward large scale public obscenity and casual sex as it is now. The pendulum will swing soon away from pornography, promiscuity, and the other so-called rights that have been so appallingly flaunted in recent years. It won't be long before the natural course of events will return you to the norm, and possibly on past it to a period of puritanism.

"Yes, although woefully lacking in certain essential areas, you *are* beginning to progress toward recognition of the necessity to help your fellow men. When the great spiritual revolution comes and man is able to lift his brothers to the high levels to which he himself aspires, then a true utopian state will be reached. The ideal is still a long way off; and many millions of men and women will suffer tribulations before it arrives. If earth life were all there is, then this anguish would have been in vain. Fortunately earthly existence is such a small part of eternal life that the suffering undergone here is soon forgotten when progression begins."

As my personal contribution to this book, I have been trying to indicate how an individual may respond to the effort to live by James' philosophy, how feeling that today's existence is only a small step in life everlasting can inspire one to carry on with renewed spiritual vigor. Although the quality of my life is much improved since James came to me, I haven't advanced as much as I would have liked. However, I do especially relish the peace of mind that remains with me like a warm security blanket.

Aside from receiving the James scripts and managing to get them published, and learning by trial and error to use an IBM Computer word processor in order to write this manuscript *Ghost Writers*, I founded and became the first president of the Survival Research Foundation, a tax exempt organization designed to do scientific research on the survival of the human soul. It's goals are to conduct, subsidize and assist in the procuring of scientific evidence for conscious survival of the human soul or spirit after death, also to establish the results of the research as worthy of public consideration; to establish survival research projects involving scientists and professional researchers interested in areas of psychical investigation other than those already significantly explored by parapsychologists; also the dissemination of information about such accomplishments of the Foundation and others in the most constructive and sophisticated manner, because misapprehensions about our field are widespread among the public and should be corrected.

Our most comprehensive undertaking during the first phase of the Foundation's activities was the devising of a code by Clarissa Mulders, who is now on the other side, and Frank Tribbe, who is still with us. The object is for living persons to prepare a code according to certain specifications and leave it with the Survival Research Foundation. Then after their demise they will try to send a message through a medium or psychic that will break the code. The message will be some line of verse or other well-known saying. When a medium receives something of this sort, it should be sent to the current president of the Foundation, Arthur Berger, P.O. Box 8565, Pembroke Pines, Florida, 33024-0565.

I am sure Clarissa is desperately attempting to get her message through, but so far her code has not been broken. I plan also to beam up sometime in the not too distant future, so all psychics reading this, when you hear of my passing, please attempt to reach me.

What else have I been doing during this time? Aging, my dears, aging. But with a certain amount of equanimity. Many of my contemporaries do a lot of complaining. We are aware of the bad conditions James has been pointing out so vehemently, perhaps not as involved as he would like us to be but appalled enough to grouse among ourselves about them. We're mostly glad we're on our way out, and sorry for those who will be left here to fight the good fight and true.

But much of our griping is because many of us definitely think people are living too long today. Few of us have taken sufficient care of our bodies to remain vigorous, yet medical research has eliminated most of the illnesses that used to carry us off at a respectable age. Now we're left with arthritis, allergies, diabetes, osteoporosis ... illnesses that erode us away gradually, making us too physically uncomfortable for life to be truly meaningful; yet we keep on going year after year after year. If all people realized, as some of us do, that they would soon be going to a higher sphere of life and continuing cheerfully to live forever, I believe it would be easier for them to handle their present predicaments.

Sometimes I think back to my main childhood quest. When I was in my teens we lived in San Antonio, Texas, and we used to sit out in the yard at night and look at the stars. In those days before city lights took over completely, we in metropolitan areas could still see a star-covered sky, and wonder what it was all about.

Every evening in summer as we contemplated this amazing heavenly canopy I asked constant unanswered and unanswerable questions. There wasn't too much I could query aloud, because Mother and Daddy and any friends who were with us didn't know the score any more than I did. But I could talk to God in my mind, even if I wasn't sure about Him. Certainly what I'd heard at Sunday School didn't compute. I would always end my prayerful questions with, "Oh, Lord, please let me find answers that *make sense*." And that is the main thing that I have now truly found, thanks to my James. Answers that make sense to me, even when they are so overpowering that I can't comprehend them. Being relieved of the fear of death and having the belief that I know where I'm going when this is all over is indeed a great blessing.

In the meantime there is little I can do but toss off an occasional book for the pleasure of it, keep my contacts with others as lively as possible, and try to truly follow the light within my heart. How could I get too upset over any problems when receiving on my typewriter such thoughts as:

"Individually each of you will attain Ultimate Perfection. That is your joyous destiny. In the meantime I urge you to take up the challenge of directing your life and that of as many others as you can influence toward an existence totally dedicated to spiritual growth and forward advancement for yourself and your world."

With this to inspire us, we will endure. No, not endure. With the assistance of those who have gone before us and want to pass their encouraging information on to us, we will *prevail!*

James says: "There is really no reason for me to dwell at length on why we in the spirit world are so eager for you on earth to know that you live after death. It should be self-evident by now that we who are working toward our progression love all of you and want you to put this knowledge to use so that your lives on earth will be happier and your transitions easier. And think of how much work you will save us if we do not have so many unenlightened newcomers to convert

"Many people do not ever think about the possibility of life after death. But most persons who think, think at one time or another about the subject — usually without achieving any answers that satisfy them. That is why they so often put the question aside, in order not to be embarrassed or confused by it.

"The truth is that your life has been for nothing unless you survive. Why should you go through all the difficulties and torments that everyone has to endure if there is no reason for it and no result from it, other than the perpetuation of the human race? Why should the species Man be continued at all, if he came from nowhere by chance coincidence and goes nowhere? To be extinguished like a light would mean that you remembered no more and suffered no more, it is true. But it would also mean that you nevermore knew joy and love.

"No one who is aware that all men are destined to return to Ultimate Perfection can ever belittle himself or his fellows. No one with such knowledge would be able to use his authority to declare war. He would not kill or in any way deliberately harm another or do anything to hinder the perfect growth of all human beings or the world in which they live. When you think of yourself as one with God you will act in a responsible manner at all times.

"No such concerned man," says James, "will make his own causes more urgent than those of another, nor his own needs more important. Your ecology problems will resolve themselves when each person thinks more of his neighbor and his neighbor's property than of his own. Your pollution will be remedied when care for all the world's beauties and bounties is more important than gain for any individual or group. Overpopulation will recede when everyone learns not to have children until they are able to raise them under conditions as nearly ideal as they can provide. There will be no racial injustices, no inhumanity to man, when all are known to be kindred with the identical beautiful destiny.

"It is our hope that you citizens of Planet Earth will grow a great deal spiritually even before you pass into the next plane and begin your progression. It is our ardent desire that you make every effort to keep your sphere physically habitable and that you continue to live on it and enjoy it for many moons. You, by your conscious efforts to love and to think positively, and your hard work for what you know is right, can improve yourselves and all those who come in contact with you and assist your world to make its start in the direction of peace and perfect conditions for all. The fact that this will entail a good bit of effort will make some of you hesitate, but the challenge will encourage others.

"Do you want to know how to do yourself a favor?" asks James. "Whenever you have any trouble of any kind, tell yourself who you are. Stop right in the midst of your worrying and say to yourself, 'I am a child of God. I am going to live forever. I am so superior to anything negative that can happen to me that it is inconsequential. I am above worry. This situation that is causing me grief will pass away and my life will be better for having endured it without letting it conquer me. I will learn from it. I will not let it cause me anguish because one who originated as a thought from Ultimate Perfection need not ever suffer. Not as a mere mechanical automaton who believes he has no soul will I face my problems, but as one who knows his wonderful destiny. Small aggravations or large woes can not conquer me, for I am immortal!'

"What could possibly really disturb your equanimity at the start of you eternal existence when you know that it is only the first step of a journey that will continue forever? It will always be a joyful and exciting life if you think of it that way from now on. It will eventually be like that all the time, why not start on earth to appreciate and enjoy it? I know all of you can do it if you will put your minds to it. I know you have the courage and the endurance and the love to overcome all negatives and sing and shout with happiness instead. I want to see you do this with your lives from now on."

James has one final message: "As we conclude this work which combines some previously published material with much additional new information, let me thank you readers for going along with concepts that are new and strange to you. Perhaps there are others of you who are familiar with the idea of evolutionary progression after death. They will find much here to add to their knowledge, plus simple truths they may not have previously contemplated. Love and positive thinking work when they are applied, so do not neglect them just because you believe them to be naive. Those who adopt these procedures are happy and fulfilled. Try it and you will see.

"I want to thank Susy Smith for undertaking this effort. Sitting at her typewriter hour after hour, year after year, has been exhausting and wearying. It is a growth process she has hardly realized as she managed to cope with the physical effort and attempted to attain the philosophical enlightenment.

"All of us in the spirit world who have worked together to send you this information will be pleased to know that many of you are attempting to use our suggestions. Keep in mind that there are countless higher spirits who love you and will help in any way possible if you ask them. You and your fellows are eternal. You will eventually be one with Ultimate Perfection, the highest of all possible destinies, so anticipate happily your shining moments of the future. Be joyous! Be filled with excitement and enthusiasm as you welcome your magnificent fate!"

BIBLIOGRAPHY

Asimov, Isaac *Asimov on Physics*. New York, Doubleday, 1976.

Barbanell, Maurice, *This is Spiritualism*. New York, Award Books, 1959.

Bastin, Ted, *Psychic*, June, 1973.

Batzler, Louis Richard, *The Rising Tide of Suicide: A Guide to Prevention, Intervention and Postvention*. Frederick, Md., Hidden Valley Press, 1988.

Bentov, Itzhak, *Stalking the Wild Pendulum*. New York, Dutton, 1977.

Blatty, William Peter, *The Exorcist*. New York, Harper & Row, 1971.

Bohn, David, "Mind Over Matter." Thames Television Series.

Bowers, Edwin F., *Spiritualism's Challenge*. New York, National Library Press, 1936.

Carington, Whately, *Telepathy*. London, Methuen, 1954.

Cerminara, Gina, *Insights for the Age of Aquarius*. Englewood Cliffs, N.J., Prentice-Hall, 1973.

Clifford, Terry, "Shirley MacLaine's Spiritual Dance." American Health, January/February '87.

Cott, Jonathan, *The Search for Omm Sety*. Garden City, N.Y. Doubleday, 1987.

Davis, Andrew Jackson, *The Penetralia*. Boston, Bela Marsh Publishers, 1858.

Doyle, Arthur Conan, *Pheneas Speaks*. New York, George H. Doran Co., 1927.

Hutchings, Emily Grant, *Where Do We Go From Here?* New York, G.P. Putnam's Sons, 1933.

Levi, *The Aquarian Gospel of Jesus the Christ*. Santa Monica, Ca., DeVorss & Co., 1907.

Lodge, Sir Oliver, *Raymond*. New York, George H. Doran Co., 1916.

Miller, DeWitt, *You Do Take It With You*. New York, Citadel Press, 1955.

Mitchell, Edgar, *Psychic*, June, 1973.

Moody, Raymond, *Life After Death*. New York, Bantam Books, 1978.

Parkinson, Merta Mary, *Love and Laughter.* Kansas City, Mo., Frank Glenn Publishing Co., 1950.

People, May 9, 1988.

Regardie, Israel, *The Tree of Life.* York Beach, Me., Samuel Weiser, 1969.

Self-Realization, Summer, 1973.

Sheldrake, Rupert, *A New Science of Life.* Los Angeles, Ca., J.P. Tarcher, Inc. 1981.

Sherman, Harold, *Your Mysterious Powers of ESP.* New York, World, 1969.

Smith, Susy, *Confessions of a Psychic.* New York, Macmillan, 1971.

_____, *The Enigma of Out-of-Body Travel.* New York, Garrett Publications, 1965.

_____, *The Book of James.* New York, G.P. Putnam's Sons, 1974.

_____, *The Conversion of a Psychic.* New York, Doubleday, 1978.

Snell, Joy, *The Ministry of Angels.* London, G. Bell, 1925.

Sondy, Dominic P., "Back to Life." Fate, November, 1987.

Stead, W.T., *After Death.* New York, George H. Doran Co., 1914.

Stevenson, Ian, *Twenty Cases Suggestive of Reincarnation.* American Society for Psychical Research, 1966.

Talbot, Michael, *Mysticism and the New Physics.* New York, Bantam Books, 1980.

Titus, Justin E., *Eternal Progression.* Lakemont, Ga., CSA Press, 1971.

Tooke, Edgar A., "Cosmic Interaction." Sunrise, September, 1982.

Vaughn, Alan, "Channeling." New Realities, January/February 1987.

Von Reuter, Florizel, *Psychical Experiences of a Musician.* Waukesha, Wis., Cultural Press, N.D.

Walbrook, Lillian, *The Case of Lester Coltman.* London, Hutchinson, 1924.

White, Stewart Edward, *The Unobstructed Universe.* New York, Dutton, 1943.

Wickland, Carl, *Thirty Years Among the Dead.* Los Angeles, National Psychological Institute, 1924.

PREREQUISITE

Comes the day that I am free
from this constricting body,
when you, with sympathy,
and complementary phrases
bid me adieu. . .
When you flower-deck the form,
discarded, that you
thought was me; by then I'll be
beyond these mundane things,
in silver silence soaring
(without wings) through
another level of eternity,
where, in another vessel,
suitable, I will continue
learning LOVE — the mastery
of, in essence, the
only prerequisite
for entering HIS presence.

— Delma Luben

Delma Luben is an author, philosopher, and award-winning
poet, currently residing in Prescott, Arizona.

9 781583 487440